Foundations of Linux Debugging, Disassembling, and Reversing

Analyze Binary Code, Understand Stack Memory Usage, and Reconstruct C/C++ Code with Intel x64

Dmitry Vostokov

Apress®

Foundations of Linux Debugging, Disassembling, and Reversing: Analyze Binary Code, Understand Stack Memory Usage, and Reconstruct C/C++ Code with Intel x64

Dmitry Vostokov
Dublin, Ireland

ISBN-13 (pbk): 978-1-4842-9152-8   ISBN-13 (electronic): 978-1-4842-9153-5
https://doi.org/10.1007/978-1-4842-9153-5

Copyright © 2023 by Dmitry Vostokov

Managing Director, Apress Media LLC: Welmoed Spahr
Acquisitions Editor: Celestin Suresh John
Development Editor: James Markham
Coordinating Editor: Mark Powers

Cover designed by eStudioCalamar

Cover image by Eugene Golovesov on Unsplash (www.unsplash.com)

Distributed to the book trade worldwide by Apress Media, LLC, 1 New York Plaza, New York, NY 10004, U.S.A. Phone 1-800-SPRINGER, fax (201) 348-4505, e-mail orders-ny@springer-sbm.com, or visit www.springeronline.com. Apress Media, LLC is a California LLC and the sole member (owner) is Springer Science + Business Media Finance Inc (SSBM Finance Inc). SSBM Finance Inc is a **Delaware** corporation.

For information on translations, please e-mail booktranslations@springernature.com; for reprint, paperback, or audio rights, please e-mail bookpermissions@springernature.com.

Apress titles may be purchased in bulk for academic, corporate, or promotional use. eBook versions and licenses are also available for most titles. For more information, reference our Print and eBook Bulk Sales web page at http://www.apress.com/bulk-sales.

Any source code or other supplementary material referenced by the author in this book is available to readers on GitHub (https://github.com/Apress). For more detailed information, please visit http://www.apress.com/source-code.

Printed on acid-free paper

Table of Contents

About the Author

Dmitry Vostokov is an internationally recognized expert, speaker, educator, scientist, and author. He is the founder of the pattern-oriented software diagnostics, forensics, and prognostics discipline and Software Diagnostics Institute (DA+TA: DumpAnalysis. org + TraceAnalysis.org). Vostokov has also authored more than 50 books on software diagnostics, anomaly detection and analysis, software and memory forensics, root cause analysis and problem solving, memory dump analysis, debugging, software trace and log analysis, reverse engineering, and malware analysis. He has more than 25 years of experience in software architecture, design, development, and maintenance in various industries, including leadership, technical, and people management roles. Dmitry also founded Syndromatix, Anolog. io, BriteTrace, DiaThings, Logtellect, OpenTask Iterative and Incremental Publishing (OpenTask.com), Software Diagnostics Technology and Services (former Memory Dump Analysis Services; PatternDiagnostics. com), and Software Prognostics. In his spare time, he presents various topics on Debugging TV and explores Software Narratology, its further development as Narratology of Things and Diagnostics of Things (DoT), and Software Pathology. His current areas of interest are theoretical software diagnostics and its mathematical and computer science foundations, application of artificial intelligence, machine learning and data mining to diagnostics and anomaly detection, software diagnostics engineering and diagnostics-driven development, and diagnostics workflow and interaction. Recent areas of interest also include cloud native computing, security, automation, functional programming, and applications of category theory to software development and big data.

About the Technical Reviewer

 **Vikas Talan** is a senior engineer at Qualcomm (an American multinational corporation). He is the founder of S.M.A.R.T Solutions, a technical company. He also worked at MediaTek and Cadence in core technical domains. He has in-depth experience in Linux kernel programming, Linux device drivers, ARM 64, ARM, and porting of Android OS and Linux drivers on chipsets. He hails from Delhi NCR, India.

Preface

The book covers topics ranging from Intel x64 assembly language instructions and writing programs in assembly language to pointers, live debugging, and static binary analysis of compiled C and C++ code.

Diagnostics of core memory dumps, live and postmortem debugging of Linux applications, services, and systems, memory forensics, malware, and vulnerability analysis require an understanding of x64 Intel assembly language and how C and C++ compilers generate code, including memory layout and pointers. This book is about background knowledge and practical foundations that are needed to understand internal Linux program structure and behavior, start working with the GDB debugger, and use it for disassembly and reversing. It consists of practical step-by-step exercises of increasing complexity with explanations and many diagrams, including some necessary background topics.

By the end of the book, you will have a solid understanding of how Linux C and C++ compilers generate binary code. In addition, you will be able to analyze such code confidently, understand stack memory usage, and reconstruct original C/C++ code.

The book will be useful for

- Software technical support and escalation engineers

- Software engineers coming from JVM background

- Software testers

- Engineers coming from non-Linux environments, for example, Windows or Mac OS X

- Linux C/C++ software engineers without assembly language background

- Security researchers without assembly language background

- Beginners learning Linux software reverse engineering techniques

This book can also be used as an x64 assembly language and Linux debugging supplement for relevant undergraduate-level courses.

Source Code

All source code used in this book can be downloaded from github.com/apress/linux-debugging-disassembling-reversing.

CHAPTER 1

Memory, Registers, and Simple Arithmetic

Memory and Registers Inside an Idealized Computer

Computer memory consists of a sequence of memory cells, and each cell has a unique address (location). Every cell contains a "number." We refer to these "numbers" as contents at addresses (locations). Because memory access is slower than arithmetic instructions, there are so-called registers to speed up complex operations that require memory to store temporary results. We can also think about them as stand-alone memory cells. The name of a register is its address. Figure 1-1 illustrates this concept.

© Dmitry Vostokov 2023
D. Vostokov, *Foundations of Linux Debugging, Disassembling, and Reversing*,
https://doi.org/10.1007/978-1-4842-9153-5_1

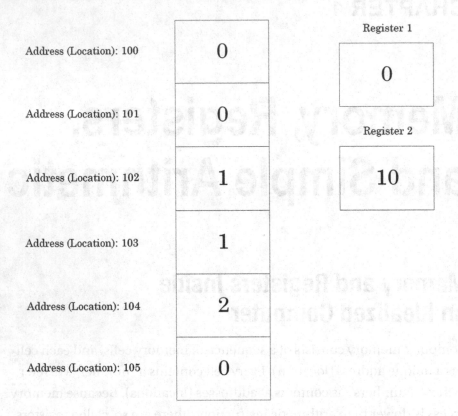

Figure 1-1. Computer memory represented as a sequence of memory cells and locations

Memory and Registers Inside Intel 64-Bit PC

Figure 1-2 shows addresses for memory locations containing integer values usually differ by four or eight, and we also show two registers called %RAX and %RDX. The first halves of them are called %EAX and %EDX.

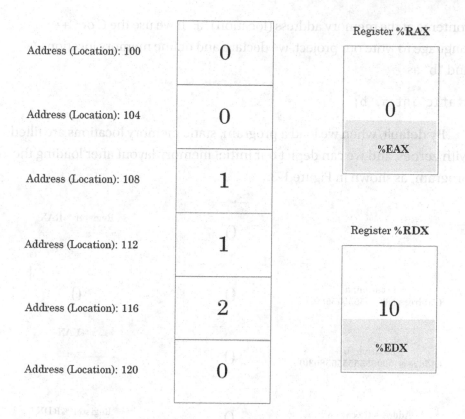

Figure 1-2. *Typical Intel x64 memory and register layout*

Because memory cells contain "numbers," we start with simple arithmetic and ask a PC to compute the sum of two numbers to see how memory and registers change their values.

"Arithmetic" Project: Memory Layout and Registers

For our project, we have two memory addresses (locations) that we call "a" and "b." We can think about "a" and "b" as names of their respective addresses (locations). Now we introduce a special notation where (a) means

3

contents at the memory address (location) "a." If we use the C or C++ language to write our project, we declare and define memory locations "a" and "b" as

```
static int a, b;
```

By default, when we load a program, static memory locations are filled with zeroes, and we can depict our initial memory layout after loading the program, as shown in Figure 1-3.

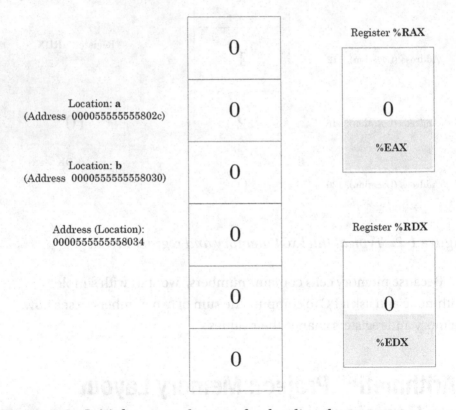

Figure 1-3. *Initial memory layout after loading the program*

"Arithmetic" Project: A Computer Program

We can think of a computer program as a sequence of instructions for the manipulation of contents of memory cells and registers. For example, addition operation: add the contents of memory cell №12 to the contents of memory cell №14. In our pseudo-code, we can write

```
(14) + (12) -> (14)
```

Our first program in pseudo-code is shown on the left of the table:

`1 -> (a)`	Here, we put assembly instructions corresponding
`1 -> (b)`	to pseudo-code.
`(b) + (a) -> (b)`	
`(a) + 1 -> (a)`	
`(b) * (a) -> (b)`	

"->" means moving (assigning) the new value to the contents of a memory location (address). ";" is a comment sign, and the rest of the line is a comment. "=" shows the current value at a memory location (address).

To remind, a code written in a high-level programming language is translated to a machine language by a compiler. However, the machine language can be readable if its digital codes are represented in some mnemonic system called assembly language. For example, **INC a** is increment by one of what is stored at a memory location "a."

"Arithmetic" Project: Assigning Numbers to Memory Locations

We remind that "a" means location (address) of the memory cell, and it is also the name of the location (address) 000055555555802c (see Figure 1-3). (a) means the contents (number) stored at the address "a."

If we use the C or C++ language, "a" is called "the variable a," and we write the assignment as

```
a = 1;
```

In the Intel assembly language, we write

```
mov $1, a
```

In the GDB disassembly output, we see the following code where the variable "a" and address are shown in comments:

```
movl    $0x1,0x2ef2(%rip)        # 0x55555555802c <a>
```

We show the translation of our pseudo-code into assembly language in the right column:

```
1 -> (a)            ; (a) = 1    movl $1, a
1 -> (b)            ; (b) = 1    movl $1, b
(b) + (a) -> (b)
(a) + 1 -> (a)
(b) * (a) -> (b)
```

Notice **movl** instructions instead of **mov**. This is because "a" and "b" can point to both 32-bit (like %EAX or %EDX registers) and 64-bit memory cells (like %RAX and %RDX registers). In the registers' case, it is clear from their names whether we use 64-bit %RAX or 32-bit %EAX. But in the case of memory addresses "a" and "b," it is not clear whether they refer to 64-bit or 32-bit cells. We use **movl** to disambiguate and show that we use 32-bit memory cells that are enough to hold integers from 0 to 4294967295.

0x2ef2(%rip) is how the compiler generates code to calculate the address "a" instead of specifying it directly. Such code requires less memory space. We explain this in later chapters.

Literal constants have the **$** prefix, for example, $0x1. The **0x** prefix means the following number is hexadecimal. The leading four zeroes of the address are also omitted in the comment. We explain such numbers in Chapter 3. Please also notice that the movement direction is the same in both the disassembly output and the pseudo-code: from left to right.

After executing the first two assembly language instructions, we have the memory layout shown in Figure 1-4.

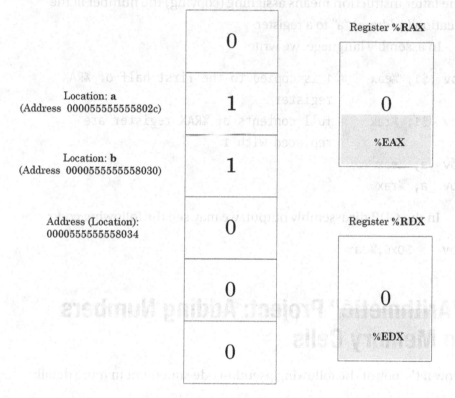

Figure 1-4. *Memory layout after executing the first two assembly language instructions*

Assigning Numbers to Registers

This is similar to memory assignments. We can write in pseudo-code:

```
1 -> register
(a) -> register
```

Note that we do not use brackets when we refer to register contents. The latter instruction means assigning (copying) the number at the location (address) "a" to a register.

In assembly language, we write

```
mov  $1, %eax   # 1 is copied to the first half of %RAX
                  register
mov  $1, %rax   # full contents of %RAX register are
                  replaced with 1
mov  a, %eax
mov  a, %rax
```

In the GDB disassembly output, we may see the following code:

```
mov     $0x0,%eax
```

"Arithmetic" Project: Adding Numbers to Memory Cells

Now let's look at the following pseudo-code statement in more detail:

```
(b) + (a) -> (b)
```

To recall, "a" and "b" mean the names of locations (addresses) 000055555555802c and 0000555555558030, respectively (see Figure 1-4). (a) and (b) mean contents at addresses "a" and "b," respectively, simply some numbers stored there.

In the C or C++ language, we write the following statement:

```
b = b + a;
b += a;
```

In assembly language, we use the instruction ADD. Because of AMD64 and Intel EM64T architecture's limitations, we cannot use both memory addresses in one step (instruction), for example, **add a, b**. We can only use the **add register, b** instruction to add the value stored in the **register** to the contents of the memory cell **b**. Recall that a register is like a temporary memory cell itself here:

```
(a) -> register
(b) + register -> (b)
```

Alternatively, we can use two registers:

```
(a) -> register1
(b) -> register2
register2 + register1 -> register2
register2 -> (b)
```

In assembly language, we write

```
mov a, %eax
add %eax, b
```

or we can add two registers and move the result to the memory cell **b**:

```
mov b, %edx
mov a, %eax
add %edx, %eax
mov %eax, b
```

In the GDB disassembly output, we may see the following code:

```
mov    0x2ee6(%rip),%edx          # 0x555555558030 <b>
mov    0x2edc(%rip),%eax          # 0x55555555802c <a>
add    %edx,%eax
mov    %eax,0x2ed8(%rip)          # 0x555555558030 <b>
```

Now we can translate our pseudo-code into assembly language:

1 -> (a)	; (a) = 1	movl $1, a
1 -> (b)	; (b) = 1	movl $1, b
(b) + (a) -> (b)	; %eax = 1	mov a, %eax
	; %edx = 1	mov b, %edx
	; %eax = 2	add %edx, %eax
	; **(b) = 2**	mov %eax, b
(a) + 1 -> (a)		
(b) * (a) -> (b)		

After the execution of ADD and MOV instructions, we have the memory layout illustrated in Figure 1-5.

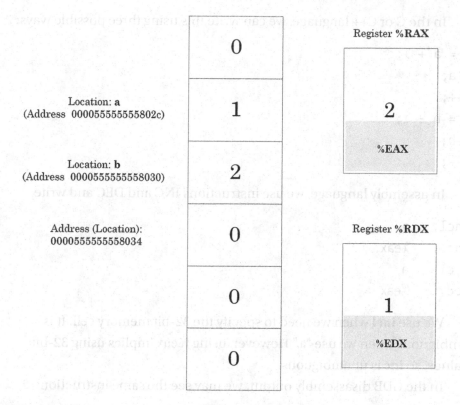

Figure 1-5. *Memory layout after executing ADD and MOV instructions*

Incrementing/Decrementing Numbers in Memory and Registers

In pseudo-code, it looks simple and means increment (decrement) a number stored at the location (address) "a":

(a) + 1 -> (a)
(a) - 1 -> (a)

In the C or C++ language, we can write this using three possible ways:

```
a = a + 1;
++a;
a++;
b = b - 1;
--b;
b--;
```

In assembly language, we use instructions INC and DEC and write

```
incl    a
inc     %eax
decl    a
dec     %eax
```

We use **incl** when we need to specify the 32-bit memory cell. It is ambiguous when we use "a." However, using %eax implies using 32-bit values, so **inc** is unambiguous.

In the GDB disassembly output, we may see the same instruction:

```
inc     %eax
```

or

```
add     $0x1,%eax   # a compiler may decide to use ADD
                      instead of INC
```

Now we add the assembly language translation of increment:

---

1 -> (a)	; (a) = 1	movl $1, a
1 -> (b)	; (b) = 1	movl $1, b
(b) + (a) -> (b)	; %eax = 1	mov a, %eax
	; %edx = 1	mov b, %edx
	; %eax = 2	add %edx, %eax
	; (b) = 2	mov %eax, b
(a) + 1 -> (a)	**; %eax = 1**	**mov a, %eax**
	; %eax = 2	**add $1, %eax**
	; (a) = 2	**mov %eax, a**
(b) * (a) -> (b)		

After the execution of INC or ADD instruction, we have the memory layout illustrated in Figure 1-6.

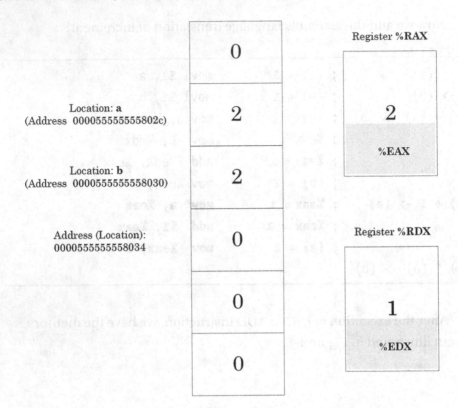

Figure 1-6. *Memory layout after the execution of INC or ADD instruction*

Multiplying Numbers

In pseudo-code, we write

(b) * (a) -> (b)

It means that we multiply the number at the location (address) "b" by the number at the location (address) "a."

In the C or C++ language, we can write that using two ways:

b = b * a;
b *= a;

14

In assembly language, we use instruction IMUL (Integer MULtiply) and write

```
mov   a, %eax
imul  b, %eax
mov   %eax, b
```

The multiplication instruction means (b) * %eax -> %eax, and we must put the contents of "a" into %EAX. The multiplication result is put into the register %EAX, and its contents are saved at the location (address) "b." Alternatively, we may put all multiplication operands into registers:

```
mov   a, %eax
mov   b, %edx
imul %edx, %eax
mov   %eax, b
```

In the GDB disassembly output, we may see the following code:

```
mov    0x2ec3(%rip),%edx      # 0x555555558030 <b>
mov    0x2eb9(%rip),%eax      # 0x55555555802c <a>
imul   %edx,%eax
mov    %eax,0x2eb4(%rip)      # 0x555555558030 <b>
```

Now we add two additional assembly instructions to our pseudo-code assembly language translation:

1 -> (a)	; (a) = 1	movl $1, a
1 -> (b)	; (b) = 1	movl $1, b
(b) + (a) -> (b)	; %eax = 1	mov a, %eax
	; %edx = 1	mov b, %edx
	; %eax = 2	add %edx, %eax
	; (b) = 2	mov %eax, b
(a) + 1 -> (a)	; %eax = 1	mov a, %eax
	; %eax = 2	add $1, %eax
	; (a) = 2	mov %eax, a
(b) * (a) -> (b)	**; %edx = 2**	**mov b, %edx**
	; %eax = 2	**mov a, %eax**
	; %eax = 4	**imul %edx, %eax**
	; (b) = 4	**mov %eax, b**

After the execution of IMUL and MOV instructions, we have the memory layout illustrated in Figure 1-7.

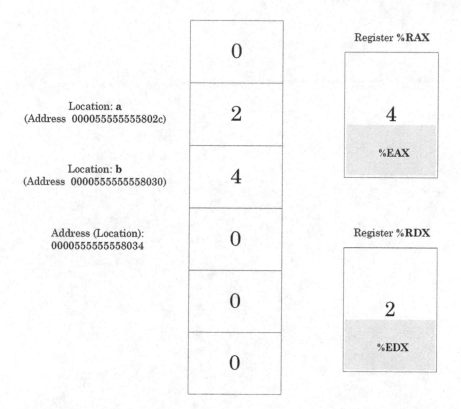

Figure 1-7. *Memory layout after the execution of IMUL and MOV instructions*

Summary

This chapter introduced CPU registers and explained the memory layout of a simple arithmetic program. We learned basic x64 instructions and manually translated simple C and C++ code to assembly language.

The next chapter looks at assembly language code produced by a debugger via disassembling binary code. Then, we reverse it to C and C++ code. We also compare the disassembly output of nonoptimized code to optimized code.

CHAPTER 2

Code Optimization

"Arithmetic" Project: C/C++ Program

Let's rewrite our "Arithmetic" program in C/C++. Corresponding assembly language instructions are put in comments:

```
int a, b;

int main(int argc, char* argv[])
{
        a = 1;                  // movl $1, a

        b = 1;                  // movl $1, b

        b = b + a;              // mov  a, %eax
                                // mov  b, %edx
                                // add  %edx, %eax
                                // mov  %eax, b

        ++a;                    // mov  a, %eax
                                // add  $1, %eax
                                // mov  %eax, a
```

```
    b = b * a;              // mov  b, %edx
                            // mov  a, %eax
                            // imul %edx, %eax
                            // mov  %eax, b

                            // results: (a) = 2 and (b) = 4

    return 0;
}
```

Downloading GDB

We used WSL2 and "Debian GNU/Linux 10 (buster)" as a working environment. We chose Debian because we used it for the "Accelerated Linux Core Dump Analysis" training course.[1] After installing Debian, we need to install essential build tools and GDB:

```
sudo apt install build-essential
sudo apt install gdb
```

You may also need to download git to clone source code:

```
sudo apt install git
cd ~
git clone github.com/apress/linux-debugging-disassembling-
reversing .
```

GDB Disassembly Output – No Optimization

The source code can be downloaded from the following location:
    github.com/apress/linux-debugging-disassembling-reversing/
Chapter2/

---

[1] www.dumpanalysis.org/accelerated-linux-core-dump-analysis-book

If we compile and link the program in no optimization mode (default):

```
coredump@DESKTOP-IS6V2LO:~/pflddr/x64/Chapter2$ gcc
ArithmeticProjectC.cpp -o ArithmeticProjectC
```

we get the binary executable module we can load in GDB and inspect assembly code.

First, we run GDB with the program as a parameter:

```
coredump@DESKTOP-IS6V2LO:~/pflddr/x64/Chapter2$ gdb ./
ArithmeticProjectC
GNU gdb (Debian 8.2.1-2+b3) 8.2.1
Copyright (C) 2018 Free Software Foundation, Inc.
License GPLv3+: GNU GPL version 3 or later <http://gnu.org/
licenses/gpl.html>
This is free software: you are free to change and
redistribute it.
There is NO WARRANTY, to the extent permitted by law.
Type "show copying" and "show warranty" for details.
This GDB was configured as "x86_64-linux-gnu".
Type "show configuration" for configuration details.
For bug reporting instructions, please see:
<http://www.gnu.org/software/gdb/bugs/>.
Find the GDB manual and other documentation resources
online at:
    <http://www.gnu.org/software/gdb/documentation/>.

For help, type "help".
Type "apropos word" to search for commands related to "word"...
Reading symbols from ./ArithmeticProjectC...(no debugging
symbols found)...done.
(gdb)
```

Next, we put a breakpoint at our *main* C/C++ function to allow the program execution to stop at that point and give us a chance to inspect memory and registers. Symbolic names/function names like "main" can be used instead of code memory locations:

```
(gdb) break main
Breakpoint 1 at 0x1129
```

Then we start execution of the program (let it **run**). The program then stops at the previously set breakpoint:

```
(gdb) run
Starting program: /home/coredump/pflddr/x64/Chapter2/
ArithmeticProjectC

Breakpoint 1, 0x0000555555555129 in main ()
```

Now we **disass**emble the *main* function:

```
(gdb) disass main
Dump of assembler code for function main:
   0x0000555555555125 <+0>:    push   %rbp
   0x0000555555555126 <+1>:    mov    %rsp,%rbp
=> 0x0000555555555129 <+4>:    mov    %edi,-0x4(%rbp)
   0x000055555555512c <+7>:    mov    %rsi,-0x10(%rbp)
   0x0000555555555130 <+11>:   movl   $0x1,0x2ef2(%rip)
   # 0x55555555802c <a>
   0x000055555555513a <+21>:   movl   $0x1,0x2eec(%rip)
   # 0x555555558030 <b>
   0x0000555555555144 <+31>:   mov    0x2ee6(%rip),%edx
   # 0x555555558030 <b>
   0x000055555555514a <+37>:   mov    0x2edc(%rip),%eax
   # 0x55555555802c <a>
   0x0000555555555150 <+43>:   add    %edx,%eax
```

```
0x0000555555555152 <+45>:      mov     %eax,0x2ed8(%rip)
# 0x555555558030 <b>
0x0000555555555158 <+51>:      mov     0x2ece(%rip),%eax
# 0x55555555802c <a>
0x000055555555515e <+57>:      add     $0x1,%eax
0x0000555555555161 <+60>:      mov     %eax,0x2ec5(%rip)
# 0x55555555802c <a>
0x0000555555555167 <+66>:      mov     0x2ec3(%rip),%edx
# 0x555555558030 <b>
0x000055555555516d <+72>:      mov     0x2eb9(%rip),%eax
# 0x55555555802c <a>
0x0000555555555173 <+78>:      imul    %edx,%eax
0x0000555555555176 <+81>:      mov     %eax,0x2eb4(%rip)
# 0x555555558030 <b>
0x000055555555517c <+87>:      mov     $0x0,%eax
0x0000555555555181 <+92>:      pop     %rbp
0x0000555555555182 <+93>:      retq
End of assembler dump.
```

We repeat the part of the formatted disassembly output here that corresponds to our C/C++ code:

```
0x0000555555555130 <+11>:      movl    $0x1,0x2ef2(%rip)
# 0x55555555802c <a>
0x000055555555513a <+21>:      movl    $0x1,0x2eec(%rip)
# 0x555555558030 <b>
0x0000555555555144 <+31>:      mov     0x2ee6(%rip),%edx
# 0x555555558030 <b>
0x000055555555514a <+37>:      mov     0x2edc(%rip),%eax
# 0x55555555802c <a>
0x0000555555555150 <+43>:      add     %edx,%eax
```

```
0x0000555555555152 <+45>:    mov    %eax,0x2ed8(%rip)
# 0x555555558030 <b>
0x0000555555555158 <+51>:    mov    0x2ece(%rip),%eax
# 0x55555555802c <a>
0x000055555555515e <+57>:    add    $0x1,%eax
0x0000555555555161 <+60>:    mov    %eax,0x2ec5(%rip)
# 0x55555555802c <a>
0x0000555555555167 <+66>:    mov    0x2ec3(%rip),%edx
# 0x555555558030 <b>
0x000055555555516d <+72>:    mov    0x2eb9(%rip),%eax
# 0x55555555802c <a>
0x0000555555555173 <+78>:    imul   %edx,%eax
0x0000555555555176 <+81>:    mov    %eax,0x2eb4(%rip)
# 0x555555558030 <b>
```

We can directly translate it to bare assembly code we used in the previous chapter and put corresponding pseudo-code in comments:

```
movl    $1, a               # 1 -> (a)
movl    $1, b               # 1 -> (b)
mov     b, %edx             # (b) + (a) -> (b)
mov     a, %eax
add     %edx, %eax
mov     %eax, b
mov     a, %eax             # (a) + 1 -> (a)
add     $1, %eax
mov     %eax, a
mov     b, %edx             # (b) * (a) -> (b)
mov     a, %eax
imul    %edx, %eax
mov     %eax, b
```

Now we can exit GDB:

```
(gdb) q
A debugging session is active.

        Inferior 1 [process 2249] will be killed.

Quit anyway? (y or n) y
coredump@DESKTOP-IS6V2LO:~/pflddr/x64/Chapter2$
```

GDB Disassembly Output – Optimization

If we compile and link the program in optimization mode:

```
coredump@DESKTOP-IS6V2LO:~/pflddr/x64/Chapter2$ gcc
ArithmeticProjectC.cpp -O1 -o ArithmeticProjectC
```

and after repeating the same steps in GDB, we get the following output:

```
(gdb) disass main
Dump of assembler code for function main:
=> 0x0000555555555125 <+0>:      movl   $0x2,0x2f01(%rip)
# 0x555555558030 <a>
   0x000055555555512f <+10>:     movl   $0x4,0x2ef3(%rip)
   # 0x55555555802c <b>
   0x0000555555555139 <+20>:     mov    $0x0,%eax
   0x000055555555513e <+25>:     retq
End of assembler dump.
```

This corresponds to the following pseudo-code:

```
mov $2, a  # 2 -> (a)
mov $4, b  # 4 -> (b)
```

Please note that the compiler also chose to put memory cell "b" first (000055555555802c) and then memory cell "a" (0000555555558030).

What happened to all our assembly code in this executable? This code seems to be directly placing the end result into the "b" memory cell if we observe. Why is this happening? The answer lies in compiler optimization. When the code is compiled in optimization mode, the compiler can calculate the final result from the simple C/C++ source code itself and generate only the necessary code to update corresponding memory locations.

Summary

In this chapter, we looked at assembly language code produced by a debugger via disassembling binary code. Then, we reversed it to C and C++ code. We also compared the disassembly output of nonoptimized code to optimized code and understood why.

The next chapter refreshes number representations, especially the hexadecimal one.

CHAPTER 3

Number Representations

Numbers and Their Representations

Imagine a herder in ancient times trying to count his sheep. He has a certain number of stones (twelve):

However, he can only count up to three and arranges the total into groups of three:

© Dmitry Vostokov 2023
D. Vostokov, *Foundations of Linux Debugging, Disassembling, and Reversing,*
https://doi.org/10.1007/978-1-4842-9153-5_3

The last picture is a representation (a kind of notation) of the number of stones. We have one group of three groups of three stones plus a separate group of three stones. If he could count up to ten, we would see a different representation of the same number of stones. We would have one group of ten stones and another group of two stones.

Decimal Representation (Base Ten)

Let's now see how twelve stones are represented in arithmetic notation if we can count up to ten. We have one group of ten numbers plus two:

$$12_{dec} = \mathbf{1} * 10 + \mathbf{2} \text{ or } \mathbf{1} * 10^1 + \mathbf{2} * 10^0$$

Here is another exercise with 123 stones. We have **1** group of ten by ten stones, another group of **2** groups of ten stones, and the last group of **3** stones:

$$\mathbf{123}_{dec} = \mathbf{1} * 10*10 + \mathbf{2} * 10 + \mathbf{3} \text{ or } \mathbf{1} * 10^2 + \mathbf{2} * 10^1 + \mathbf{3} * 10^0$$

We can formalize it in the following summation notation:

$$N_{dec} = a_n*10^n + a_{n-1}*10^{n-1} + \ldots + a_2*10^2 + a_1*10^1 + a_0*10^0$$
$$0 <= a_i <= 9$$

Using the summation symbol, we have this formula:

$$N_{dec} = \sum_{i=0}^{n} a_i*10^i$$

Ternary Representation (Base Three)

Now we come back to our herder's example of twelve stones. We have **1** group of three by three stones, **1** group of three stones, and an empty (**0**) group (which is not empty if we have one stone only or have thirteen stones instead of twelve). We can write down the number of groups sequentially: **110**. Therefore, 110 is a ternary representation (notation) of twelve stones, and it is equivalent to 12 written in decimal notation:

$$12_{dec} = 1*3^2 + 1*3^1 + 0*3^0$$

$$N_{dec} = a_n*3^n + a_{n-1}*3^{n-1} + ... + a_2*3^2 + a_1*3^1 + a_0*3^0$$
$$a_i = 0 \text{ or } 1 \text{ or } 2$$

$$N_{dec} = \sum_{i=0}^{n} a_i*3^i$$

Binary Representation (Base Two)

In the case of counting up to two, we have more groups for twelve stones: **1100**. Therefore, 1100 is a binary representation (notation) for 12 in decimal notation:

$$12_{dec} = 1*2^3 + 1*2^2 + 0*2^1 + 0*2^0$$

$$123_{dec} = 1*2^6 + 1*2^5 + 1*2^4 + 1*2^3 + 0*2^2 + 1*2^1 + 1*2^0 \text{ or}$$
$$1111011_2$$

$$N_{dec} = a_n*2^n + a_{n-1}*2^{n-1} + ... + a_2*2^2 + a_1*2^1 + a_0*2^0$$
$$a_i = 0 \text{ or } 1$$

$$N_{dec} = \sum_{i=0}^{n} a_i*2^i$$

Hexadecimal Representation (Base Sixteen)

If we can count up to sixteen, twelve stones fit in one group, but we need more symbols: A, B, C, D, E, and F for ten, eleven, twelve, thirteen, fourteen, and fifteen, respectively:

12_{dec} = C in hexadecimal representation (notation)

$123_{dec} = 7B_{hex}$

$123_{dec} = 7*16^1 + 11*16^0$

$$N_{dec} = \sum_{i=0}^{n} a_i*16^i$$

Why Are Hexadecimals Used?

Consider this number written in binary notation: 110001010011_2. Its equivalent in decimal notation is 3155:

$$3155_{dec} = 1*2^{11} + 1*2^{10} + 0*2^9 + 0*2^8 + 0*2^7 + 1*2^6 + 0*2^5$$
$$+ 1*2^4 + 0*2^3 + 0*2^2 + 1*2^1 + 1*2^0$$

Now we divide the binary number digits into groups of four and write them down in decimal and hexadecimal notation:

1100_0101_0011

12_{dec} $\underline{5}_{dec}$ 3_{dec}

C_{hex} $\underline{5}_{hex}$ 3_{hex}

We see that hexadecimal notation is more compact because every four binary digit group number corresponds to one hexadecimal number. Table 3-1 lists hexadecimal equivalents for every four binary digit combination.

Table 3-1. *Hexadecimal Equivalents for Every Four Binary Digit Combination*

Binary	Decimal	Hexadecimal
0000	0	0
0001	1	1
0010	2	2
0011	3	3
0100	4	4
0101	5	5
0110	6	6
0111	7	7
1000	8	8
1001	9	9
1010	10	A
1011	11	B
1100	12	C
1101	13	D
1110	14	E
1111	15	F

In GDB and other debuggers, memory addresses are displayed in hexadecimal notation.

Summary

This chapter refreshed different representations of a number, including hexadecimal notation.

The next chapter introduces pointers. We rewrite our arithmetic program from Chapter 1 using pointers to memory and use the GDB debugger to execute instructions one by one and watch changes to memory.

CHAPTER 4

Pointers

A Definition

The concept of a pointer is one of the most important to understand thoroughly to master Linux debugging. By definition, a pointer is a memory cell or a processor register that contains the address of another memory cell, as shown in Figure 4-1. It has its own address as any memory cell. Sometimes, a pointer is called an indirect address (vs. a direct address, the address of a memory cell). Iteratively, we can define another level of indirection and introduce a pointer to a pointer as a memory cell or a processor register that contains the address of another memory cell that contains the address of another memory cell and so on.

© Dmitry Vostokov 2023
D. Vostokov, *Foundations of Linux Debugging, Disassembling, and Reversing*,
https://doi.org/10.1007/978-1-4842-9153-5_4

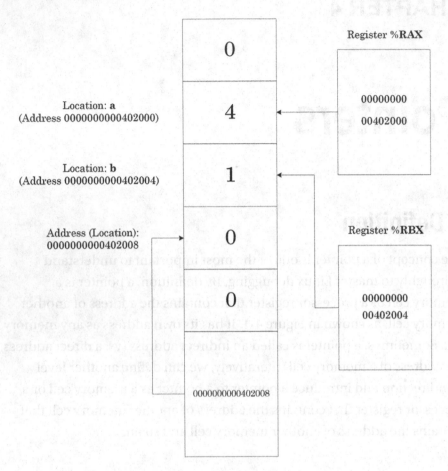

Figure 4-1. *Example pointers and memory layout*

"Pointers" Project: Memory Layout and Registers

In our debugging project, we have two memory addresses (locations), "a" and "b." We can think about "a" and "b" as names of addresses (locations). We remind that notation (a) means contents at the memory address (location) "a."

We also have registers %RAX and %RBX as pointers to "a" and "b." These registers contain addresses of "a" and "b," respectively. The notation (%RAX) means the contents of a memory cell whose address is in the register %RAX.

In C and C++ languages, we declare and define pointers to "a" and "b" as

```
int *a, *b;
```

Our project memory layout before program execution is shown in Figure 4-2. Addresses always occupy 64-bit memory cells or full 64-bit registers like %RAX or %RBX (they cannot fit in %EAX or %EBX or a 32-bit memory cell).

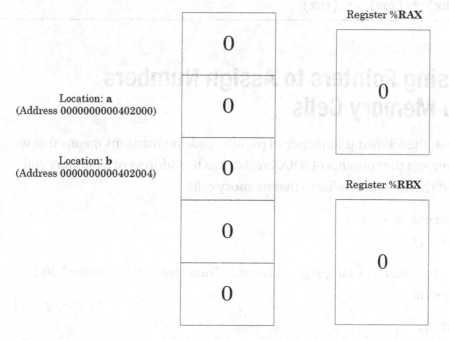

Figure 4-2. *Project memory layout before program execution*

"Pointers" Project: Calculations

In order to understand pointers better from a low-level assembly language perspective, we perform our old arithmetic calculations from Chapter 1 using pointers to memory instead of direct memory addresses:

```
address a -> rax
1 -> (rax)
address b -> rbx
1 -> (rbx)
(rbx) + (rax) -> (rbx)
(rax) + 1 -> (rax)
(rbx) * (rax) -> (rbx)
```

Using Pointers to Assign Numbers to Memory Cells

First, the following sequence of pseudo-code instructions means that we interpret the contents of %RAX register as the address of a memory cell and then assign a value to that memory cell:

```
address a -> rax
1 -> (rax)
```

In C and C++ languages, it is called "dereferencing a pointer," and we write

```
int a;
int *pa = &a; // declaration and definition of a pointer
*pa = 1;      // get a memory cell (dereference a pointer)
              // and assign a value to it
```

In assembly language, we write

```
lea    a, %rax          # load the address "a" into %rax
movl   $1, (%rax)        # use %rax as a pointer
```

Again, we see **movl** instead of **mov** because integers occupy 32-bit memory cells, and we want to address only a 32-bit memory cell. This is how it is on x64 Linux: memory cells to contain integers are half the size of memory cells to contain addresses (32-bit vs. 64-bit).

In the GDB disassembly output, we see something like this:

```
0x0000000000401000 <+0>:       lea     0x402000,%rax
0x0000000000401008 <+8>:       movl    $0x1,(%rax)
```

The source code for this chapter can be downloaded from
github.com/apress/linux-debugging-disassembling-reversing/
Chapter4/

To illustrate some instructions and not to be dependent on how the compiler translates C/C++ code, we wrote the program in assembly language. We need to compile and link it first before loading it into GDB and disassemble its *main* function as described in Chapter 2.

```
coredump@DESKTOP-IS6V2LO:~/pflddr/x64/Chapter4$ as
PointersProject.asm -o PointersProject.o

coredump@DESKTOP-IS6V2LO:~/pflddr/x64/Chapter4$ ld
PointersProject.o -o PointersProject

coredump@DESKTOP-IS6V2LO:~/pflddr/x64/Chapter4$ gdb
./PointersProject
GNU gdb (Debian 8.2.1-2+b3) 8.2.1
Copyright (C) 2018 Free Software Foundation, Inc.
License GPLv3+: GNU GPL version 3 or later <http://gnu.org/
licenses/gpl.html>
```

This is free software: you are free to change and
redistribute it.
There is NO WARRANTY, to the extent permitted by law.
Type "show copying" and "show warranty" for details.
This GDB was configured as "x86_64-linux-gnu".
Type "show configuration" for configuration details.
For bug reporting instructions, please see:
<http://www.gnu.org/software/gdb/bugs/>.
Find the GDB manual and other documentation resources
online at:
    <http://www.gnu.org/software/gdb/documentation/>.

For help, type "help".
Type "apropos word" to search for commands related to "word"...
Reading symbols from ./PointersProject...(no debugging symbols
found)...done.
(gdb)

We put a breakpoint on the *main* function, run the program until GDB
breaks in, and then disassemble the *main* function:

```
(gdb) break main
Breakpoint 1 at 0x401000

(gdb) run
Starting program: /home/coredump/pflddr/x64/Chapter4/
PointersProject

Breakpoint 1, 0x0000000000401000 in _start ()

(gdb) disass main
Dump of assembler code for function _start:
=> 0x0000000000401000 <+0>:      lea     0x402000,%rax
   0x0000000000401008 <+8>:      movl    $0x1,(%rax)
```

```
0x000000000040100e <+14>:     lea     0x402004,%rbx
0x0000000000401016 <+22>:     movl    $0x1,(%rbx)
0x000000000040101c <+28>:     mov     (%rax),%edx
0x000000000040101e <+30>:     add     %edx,(%rbx)
0x0000000000401020 <+32>:     incl    (%rax)
0x0000000000401022 <+34>:     mov     (%rax),%eax
0x0000000000401024 <+36>:     imul    (%rbx),%eax
0x0000000000401027 <+39>:     mov     %eax,(%rbx)
0x0000000000401029 <+41>:     mov     $0x3c,%rax
0x0000000000401030 <+48>:     mov     $0x0,%rdi
0x0000000000401037 <+55>:     syscall
End of assembler dump.
```

Now we examine variables "a" and "b" to verify the memory layout shown previously in Figure 4-2 using the **info variables** GDB command:

```
(gdb) info variables
All defined variables:

Non-debugging symbols:
0x0000000000402000  a
0x0000000000402004  b
0x0000000000402008  __bss_start
0x0000000000402008  _edata
0x0000000000402008  _end
```

We also verify that the values of %RAX and %RBX registers are in accordance with Figure 4-2:

```
(gdb) info registers rax rbx
rax            0x0                  0
rbx            0x0                  0
```

We instruct GDB to automatically display the current instruction to be executed, the values of registers %RAX and %RBX, and the contents of variables "a" and "b":

```
(gdb) display/i $rip
1: x/i $rip
=> 0x401000 <_start>:    lea     0x402000,%rax

(gdb) display/x $rax
2: /x $rax = 0x0

(gdb) display/x $rbx
3: /x $rbx = 0x0

(gdb) display/x (int)a
4: /x (int)a = 0x0

(gdb) display/x (int)b
5: /x (int)b = 0x0
```

Now we execute the first four instructions that correspond to our pseudo-code using the **stepi** GDB command or **si** (shorter command version):

address a -> rax		lea a, %rax
1 -> (rax)	; (a) = 1	movl $1, (%rax)
address b -> rbx		lea b, %rbx
1 -> (rbx)	; (b) = 1	movl $1, (%rbx)
(rbx) + (rax) -> (rbx)		
(rax) + 1 -> (rax)		
(rbx) * (rax) -> (rbx)		

```
(gdb) si
0x0000000000401008 in _start ()
1: x/i $rip
=> 0x401008 <_start+8>: movl    $0x1,(%rax)
2: /x $rax = 0x402000
3: /x $rbx = 0x0
4: /x (int)a = 0x0
5: /x (int)b = 0x0

(gdb) si
0x000000000040100e in _start ()
1: x/i $rip
=> 0x40100e <_start+14>:         lea     0x402004,%rbx
2: /x $rax = 0x402000
3: /x $rbx = 0x0
4: /x (int)a = 0x1
5: /x (int)b = 0x0

(gdb) si
0x0000000000401016 in _start ()
1: x/i $rip
=> 0x401016 <_start+22>:         movl    $0x1,(%rbx)
2: /x $rax = 0x402000
3: /x $rbx = 0x402004
4: /x (int)a = 0x1
5: /x (int)b = 0x0

(gdb) si
0x000000000040101c in _start ()
1: x/i $rip
=> 0x40101c <_start+28>:         mov     (%rax),%edx
2: /x $rax = 0x402000
3: /x $rbx = 0x402004
4: /x (int)a = 0x1
5: /x (int)b = 0x1
```

41

All this corresponds to a memory layout shown in Figure 4-3.

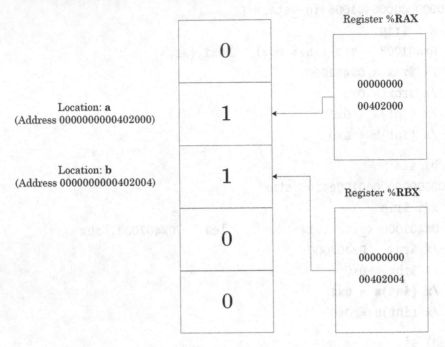

Figure 4-3. *Memory layout after executing the first four instructions*

Adding Numbers Using Pointers

Now we look at the next pseudo-code statement:

(rbx) + (rax) -> (rbx)

Recall that (rax) and (rbx) mean contents of memory cells whose addresses (locations) are stored in %RAX and %RBX CPU registers. The preceding statement is equivalent to the following C or C++ language expression where the "*" operator means to get memory contents pointed to by the **pa** or **pb** pointer (also called pointer dereference):

*pb = *pb + *pa;

In assembly language, we use the instruction ADD for the "+" operator, but we cannot use both memory addresses in one step instruction (**addl** is used to add 32-bit integers):

```
addl (%rax), (%rbx)     # invalid instruction
```

We can only use one memory reference, and, therefore, we need to employ another register as a temporary variable:

```
(rax) -> register
(rbx) + register -> (rbx)
```

In assembly language, we write this sequence of instructions:

```
mov (%rax), %edx
add %edx, (%rbx)
```

We use **add** instead of **addl** because using %EDX instead of %RDX implies adding a 32-bit integer.

In the GDB disassembly output, we see these instructions indeed:

```
0x000000000040101c <+28>:    mov     (%rax),%edx
0x000000000040101e <+30>:    add     %edx,(%rbx)
```

We add them to our pseudo-code table:

address a -> rax		lea a, %rax
1 -> (rax)	; (a) = 1	movl $1, (%rax)
address b -> rbx		lea b, %rbx
1 -> (rbx)	; (b) = 1	movl $1, (%rbx)
(rbx) + (rax) -> (rbx)	**; %edx = 1**	**mov (%rax), %edx**
	; (b) = 2	**add %edx, (%rbx)**
(rax) + 1 -> (rax)		
(rbx) * (rax) -> (rbx)		

Now we execute these two instructions (we remind that the output of the **si** command shows the next instruction to be executed when we use the **si** command again):

[From the previous output]
```
1: x/i $rip
=> 0x40101c <_start+28>:          mov     (%rax),%edx
2: /x $rax = 0x402000
3: /x $rbx = 0x402004
4: /x (int)a = 0x1
5: /x (int)b = 0x1

(gdb) si
0x000000000040101e in _start ()
1: x/i $rip
=> 0x40101e <_start+30>:          add     %edx,(%rbx)
2: /x $rax = 0x402000
3: /x $rbx = 0x402004
4: /x (int)a = 0x1
5: /x (int)b = 0x1

(gdb) info reg $rdx
rdx                0x1                          1

(gdb) si
0x0000000000401020 in _start ()
1: x/i $rip
=> 0x401020 <_start+32>:          incl    (%rax)
2: /x $rax = 0x402000
3: /x $rbx = 0x402004
4: /x (int)a = 0x1
5: /x (int)b = 0x2
```

All this corresponds to a memory layout shown in Figure 4-4.

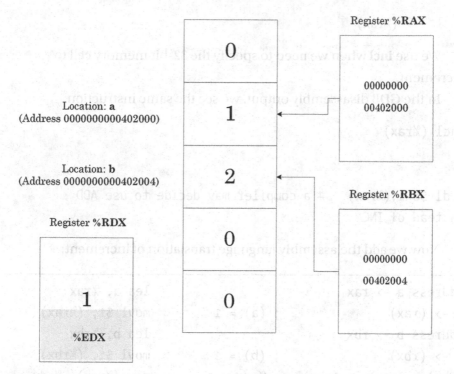

Figure 4-4. *Memory layout after executing the next two instructions*

Incrementing Numbers Using Pointers

In pseudo-code, it means increment (decrement) a number stored at the memory location which address is stored in %RAX:

```
(rax) + 1 -> (rax)
```

In the C or C++ language, we can write this using three possible ways:

```
*a = *a + 1;
++(*a);
(*a)++;
```

In assembly language, we use instruction INC and write

```
incl      (%rax)
```

We use **incl** when we need to specify the 32-bit memory cell to increment.

In the GDB disassembly output, we see the same instruction:

```
incl (%rax)
```

or

```
addl $0x1,(%rax)   # a compiler may decide to use ADD
instead of INC
```

Now we add the assembly language translation of increment:

address a -> rax		lea a, %rax
1 -> (rax)	; (a) = 1	movl $1, (%rax)
address b -> rbx		lea b, %rbx
1 -> (rbx)	; (b) = 1	movl $1, (%rbx)
(rbx) + (rax) -> (rbx)	; %edx = 1	mov (%rax), %edx
	; (b) = 2	add %edx, (%rbx)
(rax) + 1 -> (rax)	**; (a) = 2**	**incl (%rax)**
(rbx) * (rax) -> (rbx)		

Now we execute this instruction (we remind that the output of the **si** command shows the next instruction to be executed when we use the **si** command again):

[From the previous output]
```
1: x/i $rip
=> 0x401020 <_start+32>:        incl    (%rax)
2: /x $rax = 0x402000
3: /x $rbx = 0x402004
```

```
4: /x (int)a = 0x1
5: /x (int)b = 0x2

(gdb) si
0x0000000000401022 in _start ()
1: x/i $rip
=> 0x401022 <_start+34>:          mov      (%rax),%eax
2: /x $rax = 0x402000
3: /x $rbx = 0x402004
4: /x (int)a = 0x2
5: /x (int)b = 0x2
```

After the execution of the INC instruction, we have the memory layout illustrated in Figure 4-5.

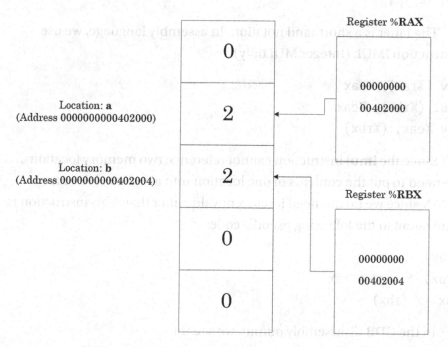

Figure 4-5. *Memory layout after the execution of the INC instruction*

Multiplying Numbers Using Pointers

Our next pseudo-code statement does a multiplication:

(rbx) * (rax) -> (rbx)

This statement means that we multiply the contents of the memory cell whose address is stored in the %RBX register by the value stored in the memory cell whose address is in the %RAX register. In the C or C++ language, we write a similar expression as the addition statement we have seen in the previous sections (note that we have two distinct meanings of the "*" operator: pointer dereference and multiplication):

```
*pb = *pb * *pa;
*pb *= *pa;
```

The latter is a shorthand notation. In assembly language, we use instruction IMUL (Integer MULtiply):

```
mov (%rax), %eax
imul (%rbx), %eax
mov %eax, (%rbx)
```

Since the **imul** instruction cannot reference two memory locations, we need to put the contents of one location into a register. We reuse %RAX since we do not need its current value after that. This instruction is equivalent to the following pseudo-code:

```
(rax) -> rax
(rbx) * rax -> rax
rax -> (rbx)
```

In the GDB disassembly output, we see this:

```
0x0000000000401022 <+34>:     mov    (%rax),%eax
0x0000000000401024 <+36>:     imul   (%rbx),%eax
0x0000000000401027 <+39>:     mov    %eax,(%rbx)
```

We add instructions to our pseudo-code table:

address a -> rax		lea a, %rax
1 -> (rax)	; (a) = 1	movl $1, (%rax)
address b -> rbx		lea b, %rbx
1 -> (rbx)	; (b) = 1	movl $1, (%rbx)
(rbx) + (rax) -> (rbx)	; %edx = 1	mov (%rax), %edx
	; (b) = 2	add %edx, (%rbx)
(rax) + 1 -> (rax)	; (a) = 2	incl (%rax)
(rbx) * (rax) -> (rbx)	**; %eax = 2**	**mov (%rax), %eax**
	; %eax = 4	**imul (%rbx), %eax**
	; (b) = 4	**mov %eax, (%rbx)**

Now we execute these three instructions (we remind that the output of the **si** command shows the next instruction to be executed when we use the **si** command again):

[From the previous output]
```
1: x/i $rip
=> 0x401022 <_start+34>:        mov     (%rax),%eax
2: /x $rax = 0x402000
3: /x $rbx = 0x402004
4: /x (int)a = 0x2
5: /x (int)b = 0x2

(gdb) si
0x0000000000401024 in _start ()
1: x/i $rip
=> 0x401024 <_start+36>:        imul    (%rbx),%eax
2: /x $rax = 0x2
3: /x $rbx = 0x402004
4: /x (int)a = 0x2
5: /x (int)b = 0x2
```

```
(gdb) si
0x0000000000401027 in _start ()
1: x/i $rip
=> 0x401027 <_start+39>:          mov    %eax,(%rbx)
2: /x $rax = 0x4
3: /x $rbx = 0x402004
4: /x (int)a = 0x2
5: /x (int)b = 0x2

(gdb) si
0x0000000000401029 in _start ()
1: x/i $rip
=> 0x401029 <_start+41>:          mov    $0x3c,%rax
2: /x $rax = 0x4
3: /x $rbx = 0x402004
4: /x (int)a = 0x2
5: /x (int)b = 0x4
```

All this corresponds to a memory layout shown in Figure 4-6.

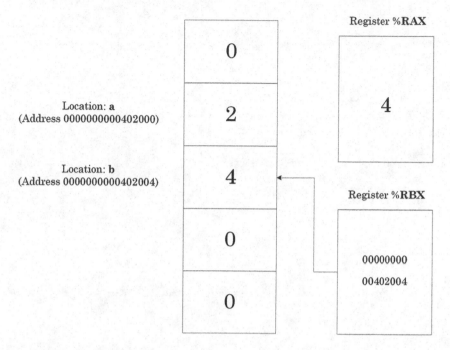

Figure 4-6. *Memory layout after execution of the last three instructions*

Summary

This chapter introduced pointers. We rewrote our arithmetic program from Chapter 1 using pointers, used the GDB debugger to execute instructions individually, and watched changes to memory. We also learned GDB commands to show the contents of registers and variables.

The next chapter introduces the bit- and byte-level memory granularity, corresponding layout, and integral C and C++ types.

CHAPTER 5

Bytes, Words, Double, and Quad Words

Using Hexadecimal Numbers

If we want to use hexadecimal numbers in the C/C++ language, we prefix them with **0x**, for example:

```
a = 12;     // 12_dec
a = 0xC;    // C_hex
```

In the GDB disassembly output, and when entering commands, numbers are interpreted as decimals by default. If we want a number to be interpreted as hexadecimal, we prefix it with **0x**, for example:

```
mov 12, a
mov 0xC, a
```

Byte Granularity

Figure 5-1 shows the difference between bytes, words, doublewords, and quadwords in terms of byte granularity. We see that each successive size is double the previous.

© Dmitry Vostokov 2023
D. Vostokov, *Foundations of Linux Debugging, Disassembling, and Reversing*,
https://doi.org/10.1007/978-1-4842-9153-5_5

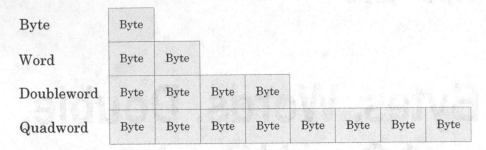

Figure 5-1. *Difference between bytes, words, doublewords, and quadwords*

Bit Granularity

Every byte consists of eight bits. Every bit has a value of zero or one. Here are some examples of bytes, words, doublewords and quadwords shown as bit strings (we can also clearly see the correspondence between 4-bit sequences and hexadecimal numbers, Table 3-1):

- Byte

  C/C++: unsigned char
  8 bits
  Values 0_{dec}–255_{dec} or 0_{hex}–FF_{hex}
  Example: 12_{dec} $0000\mathbf{1100}_{bin}$ $0\mathbf{C}_{hex}$

- Word

  C/C++: unsigned short
  16 bits
  Values 0_{dec}–65535_{dec} or 0_{hex}–$FFFF_{hex}$
  Example: $000000000000\mathbf{1100}_{bin}$ $000\mathbf{C}_{hex}$

- Doubleword

  C/C++: unsigned int, unsigned
  32 bits
  Values 0_{dec}–4294967295_{dec} or 0_{hex}–$FFFFFFFF_{hex}$
  Example: 0000**0000**0000**0000**0000**0000**0000**1100**$_{bin}$
  0000000**C**$_{hex}$

- Quadword

  C/C++: long, unsigned long long
  64 bits
  Values 0_{dec}–$18446744073709551615_{dec}$ or
  0_{hex}–$FFFFFFFFFFFFFFFF_{hex}$
  Example: 0000**0000**0000**0000**0000**0000**0000**0000**
  0000**0000**0000**0000**0000**0000**0000**1100**$_{bin}$
  000000000000000**C**$_{hex}$

Memory Layout

The minimum addressable element of memory is a byte. The maximum
addressable element is a doubleword on 32-bit machines and a quadword
on 64-bit machines. All general registers are 32-bit on 32-bit CPUs and can
contain doubleword values. On 64-bit CPUs, all general registers are 64-bit
and can contain quadword values. Figure 5-2 shows a typical memory
layout, and Figure 5-3 shows the byte layout of some general CPU registers.

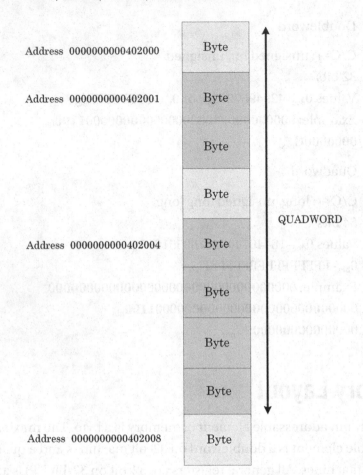

Figure 5-2. *Typical memory layout*

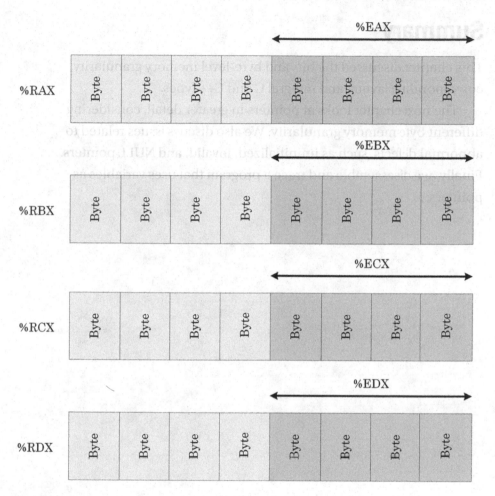

Figure 5-3. *Typical registry layout*

Remember that memory addresses are always 64-bit, and memory addresses to 32-bit memory cells like integers are also 64-bit.

Summary

This chapter discussed the bit- and byte-level memory granularity, corresponding layout, and integral C and C++ types.

The next chapter looks at pointers in greater detail, considering different byte memory granularity. We also discuss issues related to abnormal defects, such as uninitialized, invalid, and NULL pointers. Finally, we disassemble and trace a program that uses variables as pointers.

CHAPTER 6

Pointers to Memory

Pointers Revisited

The pointer is a memory cell or a register that contains the address of another memory cell. Memory pointers have their own addresses because they are memory cells too. On 32-bit Linux, pointers are 32-bit, and on 64-bit Linux, pointers are 64-bit.

Addressing Types

As we have seen in Chapter 5, memory cells can be of one byte, word, doubleword, or quadword size. Therefore, we can have a pointer to a byte, a pointer to a word, a pointer to a doubleword, and a pointer to a quadword. The GDB disassembly output in Chapter 4 has **l** suffixes in instructions involving pointers to memory that hold 32-bit (doubleword size) values.

Here are some illustrated examples:

```
movb $0xFF, (%rax)
```

© Dmitry Vostokov 2023
D. Vostokov, *Foundations of Linux Debugging, Disassembling, and Reversing*,
https://doi.org/10.1007/978-1-4842-9153-5_6

The layout of memory before **movb** instruction execution is shown in Figure 6-1, and the layout of memory after execution is shown in Figure 6-2.

```
movw $0xFF, (%rax)
movl $0xFF, (%rax)
movq $0xFF, (%rax)
```

We need to prefix 0xFF with $ to differentiate it from 0xFF as a memory address.

The layout of memory after the execution of the **movl** instruction is shown in Figure 6-3. We can see that, although we specify just a byte value 0xFF as a source operand to the **movl** instruction, it replaces all other 3 bytes of a doubleword in memory because we specify the destination as a pointer to 4 bytes, and 0xFF is 0x000000FF as a doubleword. So we need to specify the **l** suffix to disambiguate moving a doubleword value from moving a byte value. The compiler complains if we forget and use **mov**:

```
Error: no instruction mnemonic suffix given and no register
operands; can't size instruction
```

Because 64-bit (quadword) registers may point to quadword memory cells, we need to specify **q** to disambiguate moving a quadword value from moving a byte value even if we specify a constant with all leading zeroes:

```
movq $0x00000000000000FF, (%rax)
```

However, if we want to move a word value only, we need to specify the **w** suffix:

```
movw $0xFF, (%rax)
```

This is equivalent to

```
movw $0x00FF, (%rax)
```

Figure 6-4 shows a summary of various addressing modes.

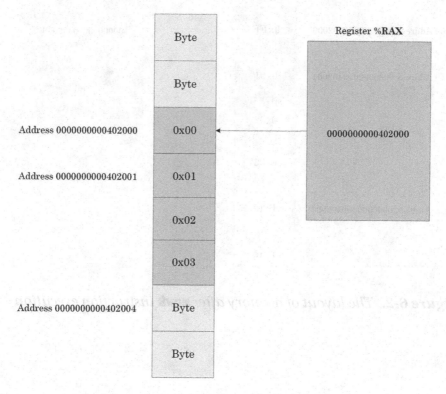

Figure 6-1. *The layout of memory before* **movb** *instruction execution*

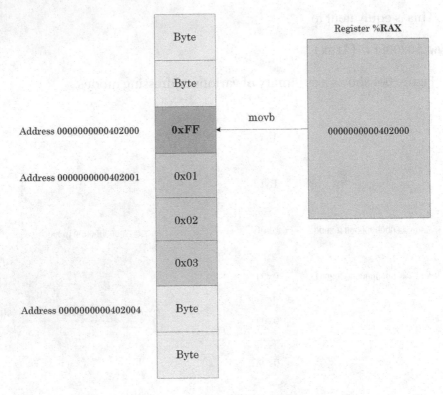

Figure 6-2.   *The layout of memory after **movb** instruction execution*

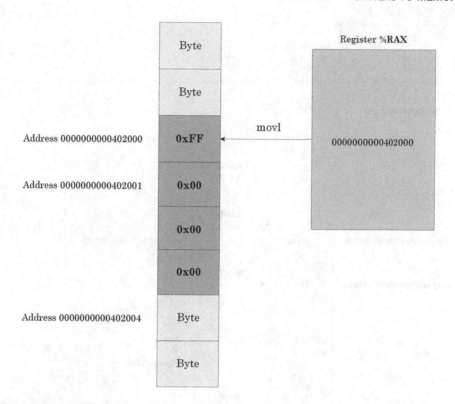

Figure 6-3. *The layout of memory after the execution of* **movl** *instruction*

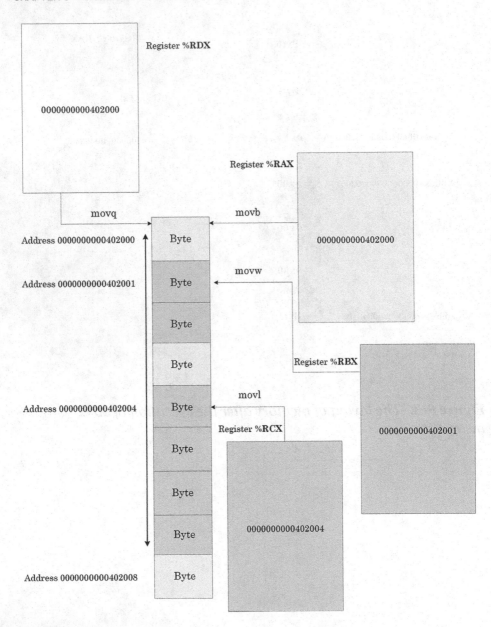

Figure 6-4. *A summary of various addressing modes*

Registers Revisited

%RAX, %RBX, %RCX, and %RDX 64-bit registers can be used as pointers to memory. They contain x86 32-bit registers %EAX, %EBX, %ECX, and %EDX. These 32-bit parts contain old 16-bit registers %AX, %BX, %CX, and %DX (each can hold a word). The %CX register was often used as a loop counter, (Counter)X, in the assembly language corresponding to simple loops in C and C++ code:

```
for (int i = 0; i < N ; ++i)
```

but modern C and C++ compilers may choose to use any other register or even a memory location for such a purpose.

NULL Pointers

Addresses 0x0000000000000000–0x000000000000FFFF are specifically made inaccessible on Linux. The following code will force an application crash or kernel panic if executed inside a driver:

```
mov $0xF, %rax
movb $1, (%rax)  # Access violation
```

Invalid Pointers

There are different kinds of invalid pointers that cause an access violation when we try to dereference them:

- NULL pointers

- Pointers to inaccessible memory

- Pointers to read-only memory when writing

Other pointers may or may not cause an access violation, and some of them are discussed in subsequent chapters:

- Pointers pointing to "random" memory

- Uninitialized pointers having random value inherited from past code execution

- Dangling pointers

The latter pointers are similar to pointers pointing to "random" memory locations and arise when we forget to set pointer variables to zero (NULL) after disposing of the memory they point to. By nullifying pointers, we indicate that they no longer point to memory.

Variables As Pointers

Suppose we have two memory addresses (locations) "a" and "b" declared and defined in C and C++ as

```
int a, b;
```

These are normal variables "a" and "b." Also, we can have another two memory addresses (locations) "pa" and "pb" declared and defined in C and C++ as

```
int *pa, *pb;
```

Here, **pa** is a pointer to an int, or, in other words, the memory cell **pa** contains the address of another memory cell that contains an integer value.

Pointer Initialization

In order to have pointers to point to memory, we need to initialize them with corresponding memory addresses. Here is typical C or C++ code that does what we need:

```
int a;              // uninitialized variable
int *pa;            // uninitialized pointer
pa = &a;            // (pa) now contains the address a
int b = 12;         // initialized variable
int *pb = &b;       // initialized pointer
```

We see that pointers are also variables and can change their values effectively pointing to different memory locations during program execution.

Initialized and Uninitialized Data

Here is a bit of additional information about initialized and uninitialized variables that is useful to know: an executable program in Linux is divided into different sections. One is called **.data**, where all global and static variables (including pointers) are put.

Consider this C or C++ data definition:

```
int array[1000000]; // size 4,000,000 bytes or 3.8Mb
```

We would expect the size of an executable file to be about 4Mb. However, the program size on a disk is only 16Kb. It is because the uninitialized array contains only information about its size. When we launch the program, this array is recreated from its size information and filled with zeroes. The size of the program in memory becomes about 4Mb.

In the case of the initialized array, the program size on disk is 4.01Mb:

```
int array[1000000] = { 12 };
```

This is because the array was put into a .data section and contains the following sequence of integers { 12, 0, 0, 0, 0 ... }.

More Pseudo Notation

We remind that **(a)** means contents of memory at the address **a**, and **(rax)** means contents of a 64-bit memory cell at the address stored in the %RAX register (here, %RAX is a pointer).

We also introduce an additional notation to employ in this and subsequent chapters: ***(pa)** means contents at the address stored at the address **pa** and is called dereferencing a pointer whose address is **pa**. The corresponding C/C++ code is similar:

```
int *pa = &a;
int b = *pa;
```

"MemoryPointers" Project: Memory Layout

This project is very similar to the "Pointers" project from Chapter 4. We have this data declaration and definition in the C or C++ language:

```
int a, b;
int *pa, *pb = &b;
```

The project code corresponds to the following pseudo-code and assembly language:

address a -> (pa)		lea a, %rax
1 -> *(pa)	; (a) = 1	mov %rax, pa
1 -> *(pb)	; (b) = 1	mov pa, %rax
*(pb) + *(pa) -> *(pb)	; (b) = 2	movl $1, (%rax)
		mov pb, %rbx
		movl $1, (%rbx)
		mov (%rax), %ecx
		add (%rbx), %ecx
		mov %ecx, (%rbx)

The source code for this chapter can be downloaded from
github.com/apress/linux-debugging-disassembling-reversing/
Chapter6/

We compile and link it and load the executable into GDB as described in Chapter 4. We get the following output:

```
coredump@DESKTOP-IS6V2LO:~/pflddr/x64/Chapter6$ as
MemoryPointers.asm -o MemoryPointers.o

coredump@DESKTOP-IS6V2LO:~/pflddr/x64/Chapter6$ ld
MemoryPointers.o -o MemoryPointers

coredump@DESKTOP-IS6V2LO:~/pflddr/x64/Chapter6$ gdb
./MemoryPointers
GNU gdb (Debian 8.2.1-2+b3) 8.2.1
Copyright (C) 2018 Free Software Foundation, Inc.
License GPLv3+: GNU GPL version 3 or later <http://gnu.org/
licenses/gpl.html>
This is free software: you are free to change and
redistribute it.
```

There is NO WARRANTY, to the extent permitted by law.
Type "show copying" and "show warranty" for details.
This GDB was configured as "x86_64-linux-gnu".
Type "show configuration" for configuration details.
For bug reporting instructions, please see:
<http://www.gnu.org/software/gdb/bugs/>.
Find the GDB manual and other documentation resources
online at:
    <http://www.gnu.org/software/gdb/documentation/>.

For help, type "help".
Type "apropos word" to search for commands related to "word"...
Reading symbols from ./MemoryPointers...(no debugging symbols
found)...done.
(gdb)

Then we put a breakpoint on the *main* function and run the program
until GDB breaks in:

(gdb) break main
Breakpoint 1 at 0x401000

(gdb) run
Starting program: /home/coredump/pflddr/x64/Chapter6/
MemoryPointers

Breakpoint 1, 0x0000000000401000 in _start ()
We disassemble the *main* function:
(gdb) disass main
Dump of assembler code for function _start:
=> 0x0000000000401000 <+0>:   lea   0x402000,%rax
   0x0000000000401008 <+8>:   mov   %rax,0x402008
   0x0000000000401010 <+16>:   mov   0x402008,%rax
   0x0000000000401018 <+24>:   movl $0x1,(%rax)

```
0x000000000040101e <+30>:      mov    0x402010,%rbx
0x0000000000401026 <+38>:      movl   $0x1,(%rbx)
0x000000000040102c <+44>:      mov    (%rax),%ecx
0x000000000040102e <+46>:      add    (%rbx),%ecx
0x0000000000401030 <+48>:      mov    %ecx,(%rbx)
0x0000000000401032 <+50>:      mov    $0x3c,%rax
0x0000000000401039 <+57>:      mov    $0x0,%rdi
0x0000000000401040 <+64>:      syscall
End of assembler dump.
```

Then we clear %RAX, %RBX, and %RCX registers to set up a memory layout that is easy to follow:

```
(gdb) set $rax = 0

(gdb) set $rbx = 0

(gdb) set $rcx = 0

(gdb) info registers $rax $rbx $rcx
rax              0x0                      0
rbx              0x0                      0
rcx              0x0                      0
```

We also instruct GDB to automatically display the current instruction to be executed; the values of registers %RAX, %RBX, and %RCX; and the contents of variables "a," "b," "pa," and "pb":

```
(gdb) display/i $rip
1: x/i $rip
=> 0x401000 <_start>:    lea    0x402000,%rax

(gdb) display/x $rax
2: /x $rax = 0x0
```

```
(gdb) display/x $rbx
3: /x $rbx = 0x0

(gdb) display/x $rcx
4: /x $rcx = 0x0

(gdb) display/x (int)a
5: /x (int)a = 0x0

(gdb) display/x (int)b
6: /x (int)b = 0x0

(gdb) display/x (long)pa
7: /x (long)pa = 0x0

(gdb) display/x (long)pb
8: /x (long)pb = 0x402004
```

We see that the **pb** variable contains the address 0x402004. We then check the addresses of (variables) memory locations "a," "b," "pa," and "pb":

```
(gdb) print &a
$1 = (<data variable, no debug info> *) 0x402000

(gdb) print &b
$2 = (<data variable, no debug info> *) 0x402004

(gdb) print &pa
$3 = (<data variable, no debug info> *) 0x402008

(gdb) print &pb
$4 = (<data variable, no debug info> *) 0x402010
```

We also check the value stored at the address 0x402004 (value of **pb** that is the address of **b**):

(gdb) x 0x402004
0x402004:   0x00000000

This corresponds to the memory layout before executing the first LEA instruction, and it is shown in Figure 6-5.

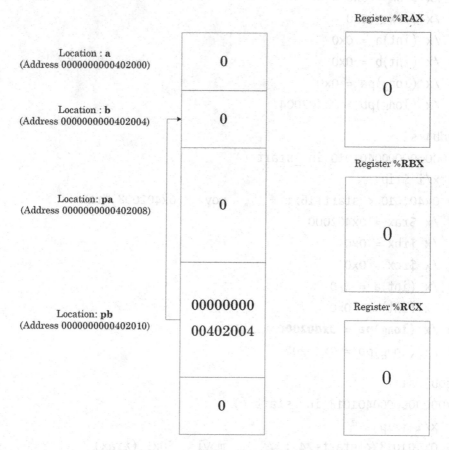

Figure 6-5. Memory layout before executing the first LEA instruction

We then execute our code step by step (changes are in bold):

```
(gdb) si
0x0000000000401008 in _start ()
1: x/i $rip
=> 0x401008 <_start+8>: mov     %rax,0x402008
2: /x $rax = 0x402000
3: /x $rbx = 0x0
4: /x $rcx = 0x0
5: /x (int)a = 0x0
6: /x (int)b = 0x0
7: /x (long)pa = 0x0
8: /x (long)pb = 0x402004

(gdb) si
0x0000000000401010 in _start ()
1: x/i $rip
=> 0x401010 <_start+16>:        mov     0x402008,%rax
2: /x $rax = 0x402000
3: /x $rbx = 0x0
4: /x $rcx = 0x0
5: /x (int)a = 0x0
6: /x (int)b = 0x0
7: /x (long)pa = 0x402000
8: /x (long)pb = 0x402004

(gdb) si
0x0000000000401018 in _start ()
1: x/i $rip
=> 0x401018 <_start+24>:        movl    $0x1,(%rax)
2: /x $rax = 0x402000
3: /x $rbx = 0x0
4: /x $rcx = 0x0
```

```
5: /x (int)a = 0x0
6: /x (int)b = 0x0
7: /x (long)pa = 0x402000
8: /x (long)pb = 0x402004

(gdb) si
0x000000000040101e in _start ()
1: x/i $rip
=> 0x40101e <_start+30>:        mov    0x402010,%rbx
2: /x $rax = 0x402000
3: /x $rbx = 0x0
4: /x $rcx = 0x0
5: /x (int)a = 0x1
6: /x (int)b = 0x0
7: /x (long)pa = 0x402000
8: /x (long)pb = 0x402004

(gdb) si
0x0000000000401026 in _start ()
1: x/i $rip
=> 0x401026 <_start+38>:        movl   $0x1,(%rbx)
2: /x $rax = 0x402000
3: /x $rbx = 0x402004
4: /x $rcx = 0x0
5: /x (int)a = 0x1
6: /x (int)b = 0x0
7: /x (long)pa = 0x402000
8: /x (long)pb = 0x402004

(gdb) si
0x000000000040102c in _start ()
1: x/i $rip
=> 0x40102c <_start+44>:        mov    (%rax),%ecx
```

```
2: /x $rax = 0x402000
3: /x $rbx = 0x402004
4: /x $rcx = 0x0
5: /x (int)a = 0x1
6: /x (int)b = 0x1
7: /x (long)pa = 0x402000
8: /x (long)pb = 0x402004

(gdb) si
0x000000000040102e in _start ()
1: x/i $rip
=> 0x40102e <_start+46>:         add     (%rbx),%ecx
2: /x $rax = 0x402000
3: /x $rbx = 0x402004
4: /x $rcx = 0x1
5: /x (int)a = 0x1
6: /x (int)b = 0x1
7: /x (long)pa = 0x402000
8: /x (long)pb = 0x402004

(gdb) si
0x0000000000401030 in _start ()
1: x/i $rip
=> 0x401030 <_start+48>:         mov     %ecx,(%rbx)
2: /x $rax = 0x402000
3: /x $rbx = 0x402004
4: /x $rcx = 0x2
5: /x (int)a = 0x1
6: /x (int)b = 0x1
7: /x (long)pa = 0x402000
8: /x (long)pb = 0x402004
```

```
(gdb) si
0x0000000000401032 in _start ()
1: x/i $rip
=> 0x401032 <_start+50>:          mov      $0x3c,%rax
2: /x $rax = 0x402000
3: /x $rbx = 0x402004
4: /x $rcx = 0x2
5: /x (int)a = 0x1
6: /x (int)b = 0x2
7: /x (long)pa = 0x402000
8: /x (long)pb = 0x402004
```

The final memory layout and registers are shown in Figure 6-6.

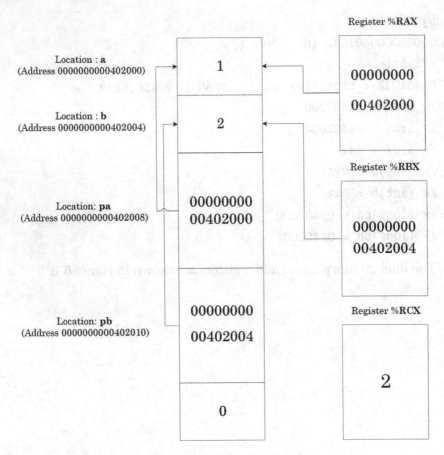

Figure 6-6. *The final memory layout and registers*

Summary

This chapter looked at pointers in greater detail, considering different byte memory granularity. We also discussed issues related to abnormal defects, such as uninitialized, invalid, and NULL pointers. Finally, in the GDB debugger, we disassembled and traced a program that used variables as pointers and learned additional commands to display memory addresses and contents.

The next chapter introduces logical instructions, zeroing memory, and the instruction pointer register. We also learn an additional GDB command to get program code and data section addresses.

CHAPTER 7

Logical Instructions and RIP

Instruction Format

We have seen that assembly language instructions have uniform format:

Opcode *operand*

Opcode *source_operand, destination_operand*

Operands can be registers (reg), memory references (mem), or some numbers, called immediate values (imm). Typical notational examples:

```
inc mem/reg
dec mem/reg
add reg/imm, mem/reg
add mem/imm, reg
```

and some concrete assembly language examples:

```
inc (%rax)
decl a
addl $0x10, (%rax)
addq a, (%rax)
```

© Dmitry Vostokov 2023

D. Vostokov, *Foundations of Linux Debugging, Disassembling, and Reversing*,

https://doi.org/10.1007/978-1-4842-9153-5_7

Logical Shift Instructions

In addition to arithmetic instructions, there are so-called logical shift instructions that just shift a bit string to the left or the right.

Shift to the left:

```
11111111   ->   11111110   ; shift by 1
11111110   ->   11110000   ; shift by 3
shl imm/reg, mem/reg
shl $1, %rax
shlb $2, (%rax)
```

Shift to the right:

```
11111111   ->   01111111   ; shift by 1
01111111   ->   00001111   ; shift by 3
shr imm/reg, mem/reg
shr $1, %rax
shr $2, (%rax)
```

Logical Operations

Here, we recall logical operations and corresponding truth tables. We abbreviate True as T and False as F.

AND

```
1 and 1 = 1    T and T = T
1 and 0 = 0    T and F = F
0 and 1 = 0    F and T = F
0 and 0 = 0    F and F = F
```

OR

```
1 or 1 = 1    T or T = T
1 or 0 = 1    T or F = T
0 or 1 = 1    F or T = T
0 or 0 = 0    F or F = F
```

Zeroing Memory or Registers

There are several ways to put a zero value into a register or a memory location:

1. Move a value:

    ```
    mov $0, a
    mov $0, %rax
    mov $0, %eax
    ```

2. Use the XOR (Exclusive OR) logical operation:

    ```
    xor %rax, %rax
    xor %eax, %eax
    ```

    XOR

```
1 xor 1 = 0    T xor T = F
1 xor 0 = 1    T xor F = T
0 xor 1 = 1    F xor T = T
0 xor 0 = 0    F xor F = F
```

This operation clears its destination operand because the source operand is the same, and the same bits are cleared.

Instruction Pointer

Consider these two execution steps from the previous chapter project:

```
(gdb) si
0x000000000040102c in _start ()
1: x/i $rip
=> 0x40102c <_start+44>:         mov      (%rax),%ecx
2: /x $rax = 0x402000
3: /x $rbx = 0x402004
4: /x $rcx = 0x0
5: /x (int)a = 0x1
6: /x (int)b = 0x1
7: /x (long)pa = 0x402000
8: /x (long)pb = 0x402004

(gdb) si
0x000000000040102e in _start ()
1: x/i $rip
=> 0x40102e <_start+46>:         add      (%rbx),%ecx
2: /x $rax = 0x402000
3: /x $rbx = 0x402004
4: /x $rcx = 0x1
5: /x (int)a = 0x1
6: /x (int)b = 0x1
7: /x (long)pa = 0x402000
8: /x (long)pb = 0x402004
```

When the MOV instruction at the 000000000040102c address is being executed, another CPU register %RIP points to the next instruction at the 000000000040102e address to be executed. It is shown in Figure 7-1.

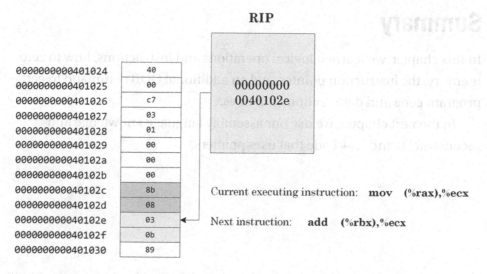

Figure 7-1. *Memory layout and %RIP when executing MOV instruction*

Code Section

Recall that in Chapter 6, we discussed the **.data** section where program data is put. The program code is put into the **.text** section.

The following GDB command lists various program sections and their information:

```
(gdb) maintenance info sections
Exec file:
    `/home/coredump/pflddr/x64/Chapter6/MemoryPointers', file
    type elf64-x86-64.
[0]      0x00400120->0x00400140 at 0x00000120: .note.gnu.
         property ALLOC LOAD READONLY DATA HAS_CONTENTS
[1]      0x00401000->0x00401042 at 0x00001000: .text ALLOC LOAD
         READONLY CODE HAS_CONTENTS
[2]      0x00402000->0x00402018 at 0x00002000: .data ALLOC LOAD
         DATA HAS_CONTENTS
```

Summary

In this chapter, we learned logical operations and instructions, how to zero memory, the instruction pointer, and an additional GDB command to get program code and data section addresses.

In the next chapter, we use our assembly language knowledge and reconstruct C and C++ code that uses pointers.

CHAPTER 8

Reconstructing a Program with Pointers

Example of Disassembly Output: No Optimization

The ability to reconstruct approximate C or C++ code from code disassembly is essential in memory dump analysis and debugging.

The project for this chapter can be downloaded from

github.com/apress/linux-debugging-disassembling-reversing/ Chapter8/

We compile and link it, load executable into GDB, put a breakpoint on the *main* function, and run the program until GDB breaks in, then disassemble its *main* function:

```
coredump@DESKTOP-IS6V2LO:~/pflddr/x64/Chapter8$ gcc
PointersAsVariables.cpp -o PointersAsVariables
```

```
coredump@DESKTOP-IS6V2LO:~/pflddr/x64/Chapter8$ gdb
./PointersAsVariables
GNU gdb (Debian 8.2.1-2+b3) 8.2.1
Copyright (C) 2018 Free Software Foundation, Inc.
```

© Dmitry Vostokov 2023
D. Vostokov, *Foundations of Linux Debugging, Disassembling, and Reversing*,
https://doi.org/10.1007/978-1-4842-9153-5_8

License GPLv3+: GNU GPL version 3 or later <http://gnu.org/
licenses/gpl.html>
This is free software: you are free to change and
redistribute it.
There is NO WARRANTY, to the extent permitted by law.
Type "show copying" and "show warranty" for details.
This GDB was configured as "x86_64-linux-gnu".
Type "show configuration" for configuration details.
For bug reporting instructions, please see:
<http://www.gnu.org/software/gdb/bugs/>.
Find the GDB manual and other documentation resources
online at:
    <http://www.gnu.org/software/gdb/documentation/>.

For help, type "help".
Type "apropos word" to search for commands related to "word"...
Reading symbols from ./PointersAsVariables...(no debugging
symbols found)...done.

(gdb) break main
Breakpoint 1 at 0x1129

(gdb) run
Starting program: /home/coredump/pflddr/x64/Chapter8/
PointersAsVariables

Breakpoint 1, 0x0000555555555129 in main ()
(gdb) disass main
Dump of assembler code for function main:
    0x0000555555555125 <+0>:   push   %rbp
    0x0000555555555126 <+1>:   mov   %rsp,%rbp
=> 0x0000555555555129 <+4>:   mov   %edi,-0x4(%rbp)
    0x000055555555512c <+7>:   mov   %rsi,-0x10(%rbp)

```
0x0000555555555130 <+11>:      lea      0x2ef9(%rip),%rax
# 0x555555558030 <a>
0x0000555555555137 <+18>:      mov      %rax,0x2efa(%rip)
# 0x555555558038 <pa>
0x000055555555513e <+25>:      lea      0x2eef(%rip),%rax
# 0x555555558034 <b>
0x0000555555555145 <+32>:      mov      %rax,0x2ef4(%rip)
# 0x555555558040 <pb>
0x000055555555514c <+39>:      mov      0x2ee5(%rip),%rax
# 0x555555558038 <pa>
0x0000555555555153 <+46>:      movl     $0x1,(%rax)
0x0000555555555159 <+52>:      mov      0x2ee0(%rip),%rax
# 0x555555558040 <pb>
0x0000555555555160 <+59>:      movl     $0x1,(%rax)
0x0000555555555166 <+65>:      mov      0x2ed3(%rip),%rax
# 0x555555558040 <pb>
0x000055555555516d <+72>:      mov      (%rax),%ecx
0x000055555555516f <+74>:      mov      0x2ec2(%rip),%rax
# 0x555555558038 <pa>
0x0000555555555176 <+81>:      mov      (%rax),%edx
0x0000555555555178 <+83>:      mov      0x2ec1(%rip),%rax
# 0x555555558040 <pb>
0x000055555555517f <+90>:      add      %ecx,%edx
0x0000555555555181 <+92>:      mov      %edx,(%rax)
0x0000555555555183 <+94>:      mov      0x2eae(%rip),%rax
# 0x555555558038 <pa>
0x000055555555518a <+101>:     mov      (%rax),%edx
0x000055555555518c <+103>:     add      $0x1,%edx
0x000055555555518f <+106>:     mov      %edx,(%rax)
0x0000555555555191 <+108>:     mov      0x2ea8(%rip),%rax
# 0x555555558040 <pb>
```

```
0x0000555555555198 <+115>:    mov     (%rax),%ecx
0x000055555555519a <+117>:    mov     0x2e97(%rip),%rax
# 0x555555558038 <pa>
0x00005555555551a1 <+124>:    mov     (%rax),%edx
0x00005555555551a3 <+126>:    mov     0x2e96(%rip),%rax
# 0x555555558040 <pb>
0x00005555555551aa <+133>:    imul    %ecx,%edx
0x00005555555551ad <+136>:    mov     %edx,(%rax)
0x00005555555551af <+138>:    mov     $0x0,%eax
0x00005555555551b4 <+143>:    pop     %rbp
0x00005555555551b5 <+144>:    retq
End of assembler dump.
```

Reconstructing C/C++ Code: Part 1

Now we go from instruction to instruction highlighted in bold on the previous page and try to reconstruct pseudo-code which is shown as comments to assembly language code.

```
lea    0x2ef9(%rip),%rax        # 0x555555558030 <a>
# address a -> rax
mov    %rax,0x2efa(%rip)        # 0x555555558038 <pa>
# rax -> (pa)
lea    0x2eef(%rip),%rax        # 0x555555558034 <b>
# address b -> rax
mov    %rax,0x2ef4(%rip)        # 0x555555558040 <pb>
# rax -> (pb)
mov    0x2ee5(%rip),%rax        # 0x555555558038 <pa>
# (pa) -> rax
movl   $0x1,(%rax)
# 1 -> (rax)
```

```
mov     0x2ee0(%rip),%rax          # 0x555555558040 <pb>
# (pb) -> rax
movl    $0x1,(%rax)
# 1 -> (rax)
mov     0x2ed3(%rip),%rax          # 0x555555558040 <pb>
# (pb) -> rax
mov     (%rax),%ecx
# (rax) -> ecx
mov     0x2ec2(%rip),%rax          # 0x555555558038 <pa>
# (pa) -> rax
mov     (%rax),%edx
# (rax) -> edx
mov     0x2ec1(%rip),%rax          # 0x555555558040 <pb>
# (pb) -> rax
add     %ecx,%edx
# ecx + edx -> edx
mov     %edx,(%rax)
# edx -> (rax)
mov     0x2eae(%rip),%rax          # 0x555555558038 <pa>
# (pa) -> rax
mov     (%rax),%edx
# (rax) -> edx
add     $0x1,%edx
# 1 + edx -> edx
mov     %edx,(%rax)
# edx -> (rax)
mov     0x2ea8(%rip),%rax          # 0x555555558040 <pb>
# (pb) -> rax
mov     (%rax),%ecx
# (rax) -> ecx
mov     0x2e97(%rip),%rax          # 0x555555558038 <pa>
```

```
# (pa) -> rax
mov     (%rax),%edx
# (rax) -> edx
mov     0x2e96(%rip),%rax            # 0x555555558040 <pb>
# (pb) -> rax
imul    %ecx,%edx
# ecx * edx -> edx
mov     %edx,(%rax)
# edx -> (rax)
```

Reconstructing C/C++ Code: Part 2

Now we group pseudo-code together with possible mixed C/C++ and
assembly language equivalents:

```
address a -> rax          ; int a; int *pa;
rax -> (pa)               ; pa = &a;

address b -> rax          ; int b; int *pb;
rax -> (pb)               ; pb = &b;

(pa) -> rax               ; *pa = 1;
1 -> (rax)

(pb) -> rax               ; *pb = 1;
1 -> (rax)

(pb) -> rax               ; ecx = *pb;
(rax) -> ecx

(pa) -> rax               ; edx = *pa;
(rax) -> edx

(pb) -> rax
```

```
ecx + edx -> edx              ; edx = ecx + edx;
edx -> (rax)                  ; *pb = edx;

(pa) -> rax                   ; edx = *pa;
(rax) -> edx

1 + edx -> edx                ; edx = 1 + edx;
edx -> (rax)                  ; *pa = edx;

(pb) -> rax                   ; ecx = *pb;
(rax) -> ecx

(pa) -> rax                   ; edx = *pa;
(rax) -> edx

(pb) -> rax
ecx * edx -> edx              ; edx = ecx * edx;
edx -> (rax)                  ; *pb = edx;
```

Reconstructing C/C++ Code: Part 3

Next, we combine more mixed statements into C/C++ language code:

```
int a; int *pa;
pa = &a;

int b; int *pb;
pb = &b;

*pa = 1;
*pb = 1;

ecx = *pb;                    ; *pb = *pb + *pa;
edx = *pa;
edx = ecx + edx;
```

```
*pb = edx;

edx = *pa;                    ; *pa = 1 + *pa;
edx = 1 + edx;
*pa = edx;

ecx = *pb;                    ; *pb = *pb * *pa;
edx = *pa;
edx = ecx * edx;
*pb = edx;
```

Reconstructing C/C++ Code: C/C++ Program

Finally, we have something that looks like a complete C/C++ code:

```
int a, b;
int *pa, *pb;

pa = &a;
pb = &b;

*pa = 1;
*pb = 1;

*pb = *pb + *pa;

++*pa;

*pb = *pb * *pa;
```

If we look at the project source code PointersAsVariables.cpp, we see the same code compiled into the executable file that we were disassembling.

Example of Disassembly Output: Optimized Program

The optimized program (compiled with -O2) contains fewer CPU instructions:

```
(gdb) disass main
Dump of assembler code for function main:
=> 0x0000555555555040 <+0>:    lea    0x2ffd(%rip),%rax
# 0x555555558044 <a>
   0x0000555555555047 <+7>:    movl   $0x2,0x2ff3(%rip)
   # 0x555555558044 <a>
   0x0000555555555051 <+17>:   mov    %rax,0x2fe0(%rip)
   # 0x555555558038 <pa>
   0x0000555555555058 <+24>:   lea    0x2fe1(%rip),%rax
   # 0x555555558040 <b>
   0x000055555555505f <+31>:   mov    %rax,0x2fca(%rip)
   # 0x555555558030 <pb>
   0x0000555555555066 <+38>:   xor    %eax,%eax
   0x0000555555555068 <+40>:   movl   $0x4,0x2fce(%rip)
   # 0x555555558040 <b>
   0x0000555555555072 <+50>:   retq
End of assembler dump.
```

We see that the compiler was able to figure out the result of computation: a = 2; b = 4. However, one question remains: Why did the compiler not optimize away the first instructions initializing **pa** and **pb** variables? The answer lies in the nature of a separate compilation model in C and C++. We can compile several compilation unit (.c or .cpp) files separately and independently. Therefore, there is no guarantee that another compilation unit would not reference our globally declared and defined **pa** and **pb** variables.

We can also see that the compiler reordered instructions. It can be seen in pseudo-code:

```
address a -> rax
1 -> (a)
rax -> (pa)
```

This is because **pa** initialization with the address of the variable **a** is independent of assigning 1 to the memory cell the variable **a** points to, and the reordered sequence of instructions could be executed faster on modern processors.

Summary

In this chapter, we used our assembly language knowledge to reconstruct C and C++ code that uses pointers. We also compared the disassembly of the optimized code.

The next chapter looks at the stack memory layout and its operations, jump instructions, and function calls. We also explore a call stack using the GDB debugger.

CHAPTER 9

Memory and Stacks

Stack: A Definition

A stack is a simple computational device with two operations, push and pop, that allows us to pile up data to remember it in LIFO (Last In First Out) manner and quickly retrieve the last piled data item as shown in Figure 9-1.

© Dmitry Vostokov 2023
D. Vostokov, *Foundations of Linux Debugging, Disassembling, and Reversing*,
https://doi.org/10.1007/978-1-4842-9153-5_9

Push operation

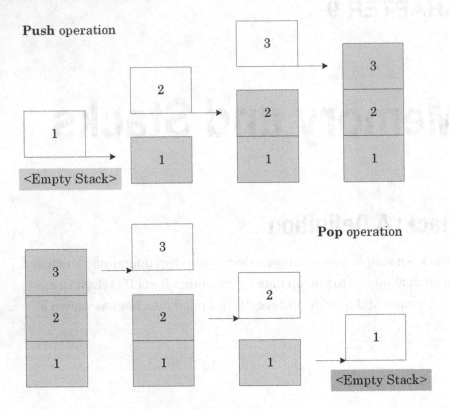

Figure 9-1. *Stack operations illustrated*

Stack Implementation in Memory

The CPU %RSP register (Stack Pointer) points to the top of a stack. As shown in Figure 9-2, a stack grows toward lower memory addresses with every push instruction, and this is implemented as the %RSP register decrements by eight. We can read the top stack value using the following instruction:

```
mov (%rsp), %rax
```

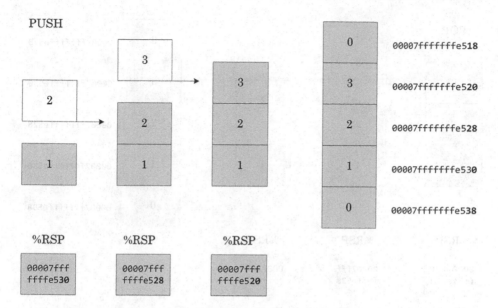

Figure 9-2. *Memory layout during push operations*

The opposite POP instruction increments the value of the %RSP register, as shown in Figure 9-3.

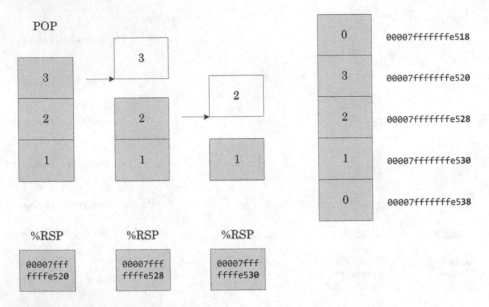

Figure 9-3. *Memory layout during pop operations*

Things to Remember

Here is the summary of what we have learned about stacks with the last three points covered in the subsequent chapters of this book:

- Stack operations are LIFO – Last In First Out.

- The stack grows down in memory.

- The %RSP register points to the top of a stack.

- Stacks are used for storing return addresses for CALL instructions.

- Stacks are used for passing additional parameters to functions.

- Stacks are used for storing function parameter values and local and temporary variables.

PUSH Instruction

We can push a value stored in a register, a value stored at a memory address, or a constant (immediate operand):

PUSH r/mem/imm

Here is a PUSH simplified pseudo-code adopted from the Intel manual:

```
IF OperandSize = 64
     THEN
             %RSP - 8 -> %RSP
             OperandValue -> (%RSP)  ; quadword
     ELSE
             %RSP - 2 -> %RSP
             OperandValue -> (%RSP)  ; word
FI
```

Examples:

```
push    %rax
pushw   (%rbx)
push    $0
```

POP Instruction

We can pop a value stored on the top of a stack to a register or a memory address:

POP r/mem

Here is a POP simplified pseudo-code adopted from the Intel manual:

```
IF OperandSize = 64
```

```
    THEN
            (%RSP) -> OperandValue   ; quadword
            %RSP + 8 -> %RSP
    ELSE
            (%RSP) -> OperandValue   ; word
            %RSP + 2 -> %RSP
FI
```

Examples:

```
pop     %rax
popw    (%rbx)
```

Register Review

So far, we have seen and used general-purpose CPU registers:

- %RAX (among its specific uses is to contain function return values)

- %RBX

- %RCX

- %RDX

We also have special-purpose registers:

- %RIP (Instruction Pointer)

- %RSP (Stack Pointer)

AMD64 and Intel EM64T architectures introduced additional general-purpose registers: %R8, %R9, %R10, %R11, %R12, %R13, %R14, %R15.

These additional registers are used a lot in the x64 code. More general-purpose registers allow faster code execution because temporary computation results can be stored there instead of memory locations. Here is a disassembly from the *read* function:

```
(gdb) disass read
Dump of assembler code for function __GI___libc_read:
   0x00007ffff7ef2450 <+0>:     lea    0xd6299(%rip),%rax
   # 0x7ffff7fc86f0 <__libc_multiple_threads>
   0x00007ffff7ef2457 <+7>:     mov    (%rax),%eax
   0x00007ffff7ef2459 <+9>:     test   %eax,%eax
   0x00007ffff7ef245b <+11>:    jne    0x7ffff7ef2470 <__GI___
                                        libc_read+32>
   0x00007ffff7ef245d <+13>:    xor    %eax,%eax
   0x00007ffff7ef245f <+15>:    syscall
   0x00007ffff7ef2461 <+17>:    cmp    $0xfffffffffffff000,%rax
   0x00007ffff7ef2467 <+23>:    ja     0x7ffff7ef24c0 <__GI___
                                        libc_read+112>
   0x00007ffff7ef2469 <+25>:    retq
   0x00007ffff7ef246a <+26>:    nopw   0x0(%rax,%rax,1)
   0x00007ffff7ef2470 <+32>:    push   %r12
   0x00007ffff7ef2472 <+34>:    mov    %rdx,%r12
   0x00007ffff7ef2475 <+37>:    push   %rbp
   0x00007ffff7ef2476 <+38>:    mov    %rsi,%rbp
   0x00007ffff7ef2479 <+41>:    push   %rbx
   0x00007ffff7ef247a <+42>:    mov    %edi,%ebx
   0x00007ffff7ef247c <+44>:    sub    $0x10,%rsp
   0x00007ffff7ef2480 <+48>:    callq  0x7ffff7f0e750 <__libc_
                                        enable_asynccancel>
   0x00007ffff7ef2485 <+53>:    mov    %r12,%rdx
   0x00007ffff7ef2488 <+56>:    mov    %rbp,%rsi
   0x00007ffff7ef248b <+59>:    mov    %ebx,%edi
   0x00007ffff7ef248d <+61>:    mov    %eax,%r8d
   0x00007ffff7ef2490 <+64>:    xor    %eax,%eax
```

```
0x00007ffff7ef2492 <+66>:      syscall
0x00007ffff7ef2494 <+68>:      cmp      $0xfffffffffffff000,%rax
0x00007ffff7ef249a <+74>:      ja       0x7ffff7ef24d4 <__GI__
                                         libc_read+132>
0x00007ffff7ef249c <+76>:      mov      %r8d,%edi
0x00007ffff7ef249f <+79>:      mov      %rax,0x8(%rsp)
0x00007ffff7ef24a4 <+84>:      callq    0x7ffff7f0e7b0 <__libc_
                                         disable_asynccancel>
0x00007ffff7ef24a9 <+89>:      mov      0x8(%rsp),%rax
0x00007ffff7ef24ae <+94>:      add      $0x10,%rsp
0x00007ffff7ef24b2 <+98>:      pop      %rbx
0x00007ffff7ef24b3 <+99>:      pop      %rbp
0x00007ffff7ef24b4 <+100>:     pop      %r12
0x00007ffff7ef24b6 <+102>:     retq
0x00007ffff7ef24b7 <+103>:     nopw     0x0(%rax,%rax,1)
0x00007ffff7ef24c0 <+112>:     mov      0xd09a9(%rip),%rdx
# 0x7ffff7fc2e70
0x00007ffff7ef24c7 <+119>:     neg      %eax
0x00007ffff7ef24c9 <+121>:     mov      %eax,%fs:(%rdx)
0x00007ffff7ef24cc <+124>:     mov      $0xffffffffffffffff,%rax
0x00007ffff7ef24d3 <+131>:     retq
0x00007ffff7ef24d4 <+132>:     mov      0xd0995(%rip),%rdx
# 0x7ffff7fc2e70
0x00007ffff7ef24db <+139>:     neg      %eax
0x00007ffff7ef24dd <+141>:     mov      %eax,%fs:(%rdx)
0x00007ffff7ef24e0 <+144>:     mov      $0xffffffffffffffff,%rax
0x00007ffff7ef24e7 <+151>:     jmp      0x7ffff7ef249c <__GI__
                                         libc_read+76>
```

End of assembler dump.

Application Memory Simplified

When an executable file is loaded into memory, its header and sections are mapped to memory pages. Some data and code are copied unmodified, but some data is initialized and expanded. The first stack is also created at this stage. The %RIP register is set to point to the first program instruction, and %RSP points to the top of the stack. This simplified process is shown in Figure 9-4.

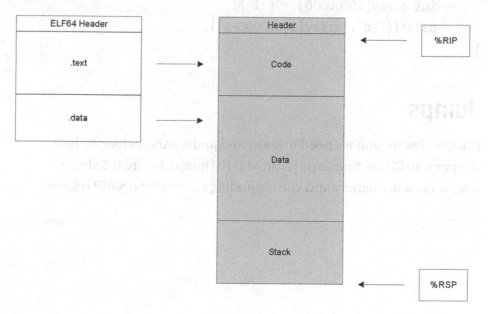

Figure 9-4. *Application memory layout*

Stack Overflow

By default, the stack size is limited (system and limit dependent, and on our system, it is 8192Kb or 8388608 bytes). If a stack grows beyond the reserved limit, a stack overflow occurs (segmentation fault). It can be caused by an unlimited recursion, deep recursion, or very large local variables:

```
int func()
{
    func();
    return 0;
}

int func2()
{
    int array[10000000] = { 1 };
    printf("%d", array[10000000-1]);
}
```

Jumps

Another instruction we need to know and understand before we look deeper into C/C++ functions is called JMP (Jump). Figure 9-5 shows instructions in memory and corresponding values of the %RIP register.

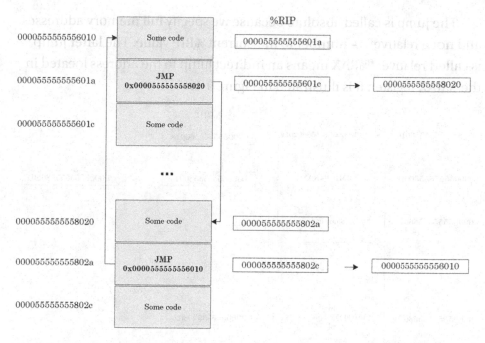

Figure 9-5. *Example memory and register layout for JMP instruction execution*

We see that the JMP instruction changes %RIP to point to another memory address, and the program execution continues from that location. The code shown in Figure 9-5 loops indefinitely: this can be considered a hang and CPU spike.

Here is a pseudo-code for absolute JMP instructions adopted from Intel manuals and some examples:

```
; Format and arguments:
  JMP r/mem64
; Pseudo-code:
  DEST -> RIP        ; new destination address for execution
; Examples:
  JMP 0x555555558020
  JMP *%RAX
```

The jump is called absolute because we specify full memory addresses and not a relative +/– number to the current %RIP value. The latter jump is called relative. *%RAX means an indirect jump to the address located in the %RAX register. It is illustrated in Figure 9-6.

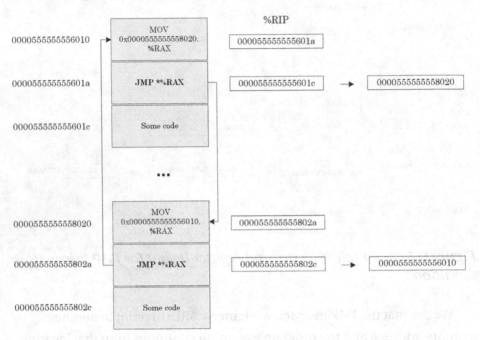

Figure 9-6. *Example memory and register layout for relative JMP instruction execution*

Calls

We discuss two essential instructions that make the implementation of C and C++ function calls. They are called CALL and RET. Figure 9-7 shows instructions in memory and corresponding values of %RIP and %RSP registers.

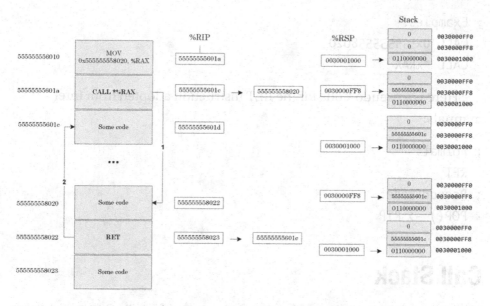

Figure 9-7. *Example memory and register layout for CALL and RET instruction execution*

We see that the CALL instruction pushes the current value of %RIP to the stack and changes %RIP to point to another memory address. Then the program execution continues from the new location. The RET instruction pops the saved %RIP value from the stack to the %RIP register. Then the program execution resumes at the memory location after the CALL instruction.

Here is a pseudo-code for CALL instructions and some examples adopted from Intel manuals:

```
; Format and arguments:
  CALL r/mem64
; Pseudo-code:
  PUSH RIP
  DEST -> RIP
```

```
; Examples:
  CALL 0x555555558020
  CALL *%RAX
```

Here is a pseudo-code for the RET instruction adopted from Intel manuals:

```
; Format:
  RET
; Pseudo-code:
  POP() -> RIP
```

Call Stack

If one function (the caller) calls another function (the callee) in C and C++, the resulting code is implemented using the CALL instruction, and during its execution, the return address is saved on the stack. If the callee calls another function, the return address is also saved on the stack, and so on. Therefore, we have the so-called call stack of return addresses. Let us see this with a simple but trimmed-down example.

Suppose we have three functions with their code occupying the following addresses:

```
func  0000000140001000 - 0000000140001100
func2 0000000140001101 - 0000000140001200
func3 0000000140001201 - 0000000140001300
```

We also have the following code where *func* calls *func2*, and *func2* calls *func3*:

```
void func()
{
    func2();
```

```
}
void func2()
{
    func3();
}
```

When *func* calls *func2*, the caller's return address is pushed to the stack, and %RSP points to some value in the 0000000140001000–0000000140001100 range, say 0000000140001020. When *func2* calls *func3*, the caller's return address is also pushed to the stack, and %RSP points to some value in the 0000000140001101–0000000140001200 range, say 0000000140001180. If we interrupt *func3* with a debugger and inspect %RIP, we would find its value in the range of 0000000140001201–0000000140001300, say 0000000140001250. Therefore, we have the memory and register layout shown in Figure 9-8 (the usual function prolog is not shown; we will learn about it in the next chapter).

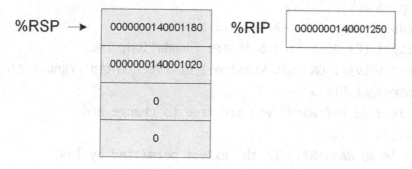

Figure 9-8. Example memory and register layout for call stack

The debugger examines the value of the %RIP register and the values on top of the stack and then reconstructs this call stack:

```
func3
func2
func
```

The debugger gets address ranges corresponding to *func*, *func2*, and *func3* from the so-called symbolic information, which may be either stored inside an executable file or in some external file that needs to be referenced explicitly.

Exploring Stack in GDB

To see the call stack in real action, we have a project called "SimpleStack," and it can be downloaded from

github.com/apress/linux-debugging-disassembling-reversing/
Chapter9/

We compile the files and load the executable into GDB:

```
coredump@DESKTOP-IS6V2LO:~/pflddr/x64/Chapter9$ gcc
SimpleStack.c func.c func2.c func3.c -o SimpleStack

coredump@DESKTOP-IS6V2LO:~/pflddr/x64/Chapter9$ gdb
./SimpleStack
GNU gdb (Debian 8.2.1-2+b3) 8.2.1
Copyright (C) 2018 Free Software Foundation, Inc.
License GPLv3+: GNU GPL version 3 or later <http://gnu.org/
licenses/gpl.html>
This is free software: you are free to change and
redistribute it.
There is NO WARRANTY, to the extent permitted by law.
Type "show copying" and "show warranty" for details.
This GDB was configured as "x86_64-linux-gnu".
Type "show configuration" for configuration details.
For bug reporting instructions, please see:
<http://www.gnu.org/software/gdb/bugs/>.
```

Find the GDB manual and other documentation resources online at:

   <http://www.gnu.org/software/gdb/documentation/>.

For help, type "help".
Type "apropos word" to search for commands related to "word"...
Reading symbols from ./SimpleStack...(no debugging symbols found)...done.

Then we put a breakpoint on the *main* function and run the program until GDB breaks in:

```
(gdb) run
Starting program: /home/coredump/pflddr/x64/Chapter9/
SimpleStack

Breakpoint 1, 0x0000555555555129 in main ()
```

The function *func3* has a breakpoint instruction inside that allows a debugger to break in and stop the program execution to inspect its state. We resume our program execution from our breakpoint in the *main* function to allow the *main* function to call *func*, *func* to call *func2*, *func2* to call *func3*, and inside *func3* to execute the explicit breakpoint:

```
(gdb) continue
Continuing.

Program received signal SIGTRAP, Trace/breakpoint trap.
0x000055555555516c in func3 ()

(gdb) info registers $rip $rsp
rip              0x55555555516c       0x55555555516c <func3+5>
rsp              0x7fffffffe500       0x7fffffffe500

(gdb) x/i $rip
=> 0x55555555516c <func3+5>:     nop
```

```
(gdb) x/i $rip-1
   0x55555555516b <func3+4>:      int3
```

We dump the **$rip-1** value because, when execution stops at the int3 instruction, %RIP points at the next instruction (**nop**).

Now we can inspect the top of the stack:

```
(gdb) x/10g $rsp
0x7fffffffe500: 0x00007fffffffe510      0x0000555555555164
0x7fffffffe510: 0x00007fffffffe520      0x0000555555555153
0x7fffffffe520: 0x00007fffffffe540      0x000055555555513e
0x7fffffffe530: 0x00007fffffffe628      0x0000000100000000
0x7fffffffe540: 0x0000555555555170      0x00007ffff7e2c09b
```

The data is meaningless for us, and we use another command variant to dump memory with corresponding symbols:

```
(gdb) x/10a $rsp
0x7fffffffe500: 0x7fffffffe510   0x555555555164 <func2+14>
0x7fffffffe510: 0x7fffffffe520   0x555555555153 <func+14>
0x7fffffffe520: 0x7fffffffe540   0x55555555513e <main+25>
0x7fffffffe530: 0x7fffffffe628   0x100000000
0x7fffffffe540: 0x555555555170 <__libc_csu_init>
0x7ffff7e2c09b <__libc_start_main+235>
```

The current value of %RIP points to *func3*, and return addresses on the stack are shown in bold. GDB is able to reconstruct the following call stack, stack trace, or backtrace (bt):

```
(gdb) bt
#0  0x000055555555516c in func3 ()
#1  0x0000555555555164 in func2 ()
#2  0x0000555555555153 in func ()
#3  0x000055555555513e in main ()
```

Summary

In this chapter, we looked at the stack memory layout and stack operations, jump and call instructions, and function call memory layout. We also explored a call stack using the GDB debugger commands.

In the next chapter, we look into further details of the stack layout of the more complex code, for example, arrays, local variables, function prolog, and epilog. Finally, we disassemble and analyze code that uses local variables.

CHAPTER 10

Frame Pointer and Local Variables

Stack Usage

In addition to storage for return addresses of CALL instructions, a stack is used to pass additional parameters to functions and store local variables. The stack is also used to save and restore values held in registers when we want to preserve them during some computation or across function calls. For example, suppose we want to do multiplication, but at the same time, we have other valuable data in registers %RAX and %RDX. The multiplication result will overwrite %RAX and %RDX values, and we temporarily put their values on stack:

```
mov      $10, %rax
mov      $20, %rdx
...
...
...                  ; now we want to preserve %RAX and %RDX
push     %rax
push     %rdx
imul %rdx            ; %RDX and %RAX contain the result of
%RAX*%RDX
```

© Dmitry Vostokov 2023
D. Vostokov, *Foundations of Linux Debugging, Disassembling, and Reversing*,
https://doi.org/10.1007/978-1-4842-9153-5_10

```
mov     %rax, result
pop     %rdx                ; pop in reverse order
pop     %rax                ; stack is LIFO
```

Register Review

So far, we have encountered these general-purpose registers:

- %RAX (among its specific uses are to contain function return values and the lower part of a multiplication result)

- %RBX

- %RCX (among its specific uses is a loop counter)

- %RDX (among its specific uses is to contain the higher part of a multiplication result if it exceeds the maximum 64-bit value)

- %RIP (Instruction Pointer, points to the next instruction to be executed)

- %RSP (Stack Pointer, points to the top of the stack)

We come to the next important register on Linux platforms called Base Pointer register or sometimes as Stack Frame Pointer register %RBP.

Addressing Array Elements

We can also consider stack memory as an array of memory cells, and often the %RBP register is used to address stack memory elements in the way shown in Figure 10-1, where it slides into the frame of stack memory called a stack frame. The first diagram depicts 64-bit (quadword) memory cells, and the second depicts 32-bit (doubleword) memory cells.

			Address of the element	%RBP notation	Value of the element
	0		0010001000	%RBP-0x20	-0x20(%RBP)
	0		0010001008	%RBP-0x18	-0x18(%RBP)
	0		0010001010	%RBP-0x10	-0x10(%RBP)
	0		0010001018	%RBP-0x8	-0x8(%RBP)
%RBP →	0		0010001020	%RBP	(%RBP)
	0		0010001028	%RBP+0x8	0x8(%RBP)
	0		0010001030	%RBP+0x10	0x10(%RBP)
	0		0010001038	%RBP+0x18	0x18(%RBP)

			Address	%RBP notation	Value
	0		0010001018	%RBP-0x8	-0x8(%RBP)
	0		001000101C	%RBP-0x4	-0x4(%RBP)
%RBP →	0		0010001020	%RBP	(%RBP)
	0		0010001024	%RBP+0x4	0x4(%RBP)
	0		0010001028	%RBP+0x8	0x8(%RBP)
	0		001000102C	%RBP+0xC	0xC(%RBP)

Figure 10-1. *Example memory layout when addressing array elements*

Stack Structure (No Function Parameters)

Suppose the following function is called:

```
void func()
{
    int var1, var2;
```

```
        // body code
        // ...
}
```

Before the function body code is executed, the following pointers are set up:

- (%RBP) contains the previous %RBP value.

- -0x4(%RBP) contains local variable var1 (doubleword).

- -0x8(%RBP) contains local variable var2 (doubleword).

It is illustrated in Figure 10-2.

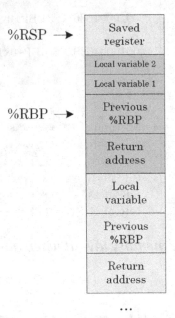

Figure 10-2. Stack memory layout without function parameters

Function Prolog

The sequence of instructions resulting in the initialization of the %RBP register and making room for local variables is called the function prolog. One example of it is Figure 10-3, where *func* calls *func2*, which has one local variable var. Sometimes, saving necessary registers is also considered as part of a function prolog.

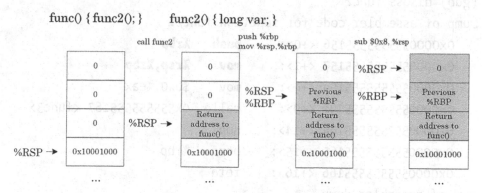

Figure 10-3. *Example memory layout for function prolog*

Raw Stack (No Local Variables and Function Parameters)

Now we can understand additional data (the previous %RBP that was equal to the previous %RSP before the function call) that appear on the raw stack together with function return addresses that we saw in Chapter 9 project "SimpleStack":

```
(gdb) info registers $rsp $rbp
rsp             0x7fffffffe500    0x7fffffffe500
rbp             0x7fffffffe500    0x7fffffffe500

(gdb) x/10a $rsp
```

0x7fffffffe500: 0x7fffffffe510   0x555555555164 <func2+14>
0x7fffffffe510: 0x7fffffffe520   0x555555555153 <func+14>
0x7fffffffe520: 0x7fffffffe540   0x55555555513e <main+25>
0x7fffffffe530: 0x7fffffffe628   0x100000000
0x7fffffffe540: 0x555555555170 < _libc_csu_init>
0x7ffff7e2c09b < _libc_start_main+235>

(gdb) disass func2
Dump of assembler code for function func2:
```
   0x0000555555555156 <+0>:     push    %rbp
   0x0000555555555157 <+1>:     mov     %rsp,%rbp
   0x000055555555515a <+4>:     mov     $0x0,%eax
   0x000055555555515f <+9>:     callq   0x555555555167 <func3>
   0x0000555555555164 <+14>:    nop
   0x0000555555555165 <+15>:    pop     %rbp
   0x0000555555555166 <+16>:    retq
```
End of assembler dump.

(gdb) disass func
Dump of assembler code for function func:
```
   0x0000555555555145 <+0>:     push    %rbp
   0x0000555555555146 <+1>:     mov     %rsp,%rbp
   0x0000555555555149 <+4>:     mov     $0x0,%eax
   0x000055555555514e <+9>:     callq   0x555555555156 <func2>
   0x0000555555555153 <+14>:    nop
   0x0000555555555154 <+15>:    pop     %rbp
   0x0000555555555155 <+16>:    retq
```
End of assembler dump.

(gdb) disass main
Dump of assembler code for function main:
```
   0x0000555555555125 <+0>:     push    %rbp
   0x0000555555555126 <+1>:     mov     %rsp,%rbp
```

```
0x0000555555555129 <+4>:      sub     $0x10,%rsp
0x000055555555512d <+8>:      mov     %edi,-0x4(%rbp)
0x0000555555555130 <+11>:     mov     %rsi,-0x10(%rbp)
0x0000555555555134 <+15>:     mov     $0x0,%eax
0x0000555555555139 <+20>:     callq   0x555555555145 <func>
0x000055555555513e <+25>:     mov     $0x0,%eax
0x0000555555555143 <+30>:     leaveq
0x0000555555555144 <+31>:     retq
End of assembler dump.
```

Function Epilog

Before the function code returns to the caller, it must restore the previous values of %RSP and %RBP registers to allow the caller to resume its execution from the correct address, previously saved on the stack, and to continue addressing its own stack frame properly. This sequence of instructions is called the function epilog, and it is shown in Figure 10-4.

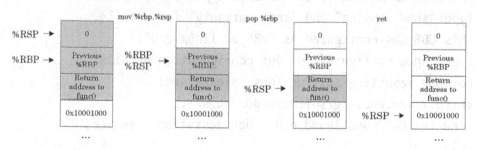

Figure 10-4. *Example memory layout for function epilog*

Instead of the **mov %rbp,%rsp** and **pop %rbp** sequence of instructions, we may see the **leave** instruction, which does the same but occupies less code space.

"Local Variables" Project

The project for this chapter can be downloaded from
    github.com/apress/linux-debugging-disassembling-reversing/
Chapter10/

We compile the file and load the executable into GDB:

```
coredump@DESKTOP-IS6V2LO:~/pflddr/x64/Chapter10$ gcc
LocalVariables.cpp -o LocalVariables
```

```
coredump@DESKTOP-IS6V2LO:~/pflddr/x64/Chapter10$ gdb
./LocalVariables
GNU gdb (Debian 8.2.1-2+b3) 8.2.1
Copyright (C) 2018 Free Software Foundation, Inc.
License GPLv3+: GNU GPL version 3 or later <http://gnu.org/
licenses/gpl.html>
This is free software: you are free to change and
redistribute it.
There is NO WARRANTY, to the extent permitted by law.
Type "show copying" and "show warranty" for details.
This GDB was configured as "x86_64-linux-gnu".
Type "show configuration" for configuration details.
For bug reporting instructions, please see:
<http://www.gnu.org/software/gdb/bugs/>.
Find the GDB manual and other documentation resources
online at:
    <http://www.gnu.org/software/gdb/documentation/>.

For help, type "help".
Type "apropos word" to search for commands related to "word"...
Reading symbols from ./LocalVariables...(no debugging symbols
found)...done.
```

Then we put a breakpoint to the *main* function and run the program until GDB breaks in:

```
(gdb) break main
Breakpoint 1 at 0x1129
```

```
(gdb) run
Starting program: /home/coredump/pflddr/x64/Chapter10/
LocalVariables
```

```
Breakpoint 1, 0x0000555555555129 in main ()
```

Next, we disassemble our *main* function:

```
(gdb) disass main
Dump of assembler code for function main:
   0x0000555555555125 <+0>:     push   %rbp
   0x0000555555555126 <+1>:     mov    %rsp,%rbp
=> 0x0000555555555130 <+11>:    movl   $0x1,-0x4(%rbp)
   0x0000555555555137 <+18>:    movl   $0x1,-0x8(%rbp)
   0x000055555555513e <+25>:    mov    -0x4(%rbp),%eax
   0x0000555555555141 <+28>:    add    %eax,-0x8(%rbp)
   0x0000555555555144 <+31>:    addl   $0x1,-0x4(%rbp)
   0x0000555555555148 <+35>:    mov    -0x8(%rbp),%eax
   0x000055555555514b <+38>:    imul   -0x4(%rbp),%eax
   0x000055555555514f <+42>:    mov    %eax,-0x8(%rbp)
   0x0000555555555152 <+45>:    mov    $0x0,%eax
   0x0000555555555157 <+50>:    pop    %rbp
   0x0000555555555158 <+51>:    retq
End of assembler dump.
```

Its source code is the following:

```
int main()
{
    int a, b;

    a = 1;
    b = 1;

    b = b + a;
    ++a;
    b = b * a;

    return 0;
}
```

The following is the same assembly language code but with comments showing operations in pseudo-code and highlighting the function prolog and epilog:

```
   0x0000555555555125 <+0>:      push   %rbp
   # establishing stack frame
   0x0000555555555126 <+1>:      mov    %rsp,%rbp
=> 0x0000555555555130 <+11>:     movl   $0x1,-0x4(%rbp)
   # 1 -> (a)
   0x0000555555555137 <+18>:     movl   $0x1,-0x8(%rbp)
   # 1 -> (b)
   0x000055555555513e <+25>:     mov    -0x4(%rbp),%eax
   # (a) -> eax
   0x0000555555555141 <+28>:     add    %eax,-0x8(%rbp)
   # eax + (b) -> (b)
   0x0000555555555144 <+31>:     addl   $0x1,-0x4(%rbp)
   # 1 + (a) -> (a)
   0x0000555555555148 <+35>:     mov    -0x8(%rbp),%eax
   # (b) -> eax
```

```
  0x000055555555514b <+38>:      imul    -0x4(%rbp),%eax
# (a) * eax -> eax
  0x000055555555514f <+42>:      mov     %eax,-0x8(%rbp)
# eax -> (b)
  0x0000555555555152 <+45>:      mov     $0x0,%eax
# 0 -> eax (return value)
  0x0000555555555157 <+50>:      pop     %rbp
# restoring previous frame
  0x0000555555555158 <+51>:      retq
# return 0
```

The compiler didn't emit the **mov %rbp,%rsp** instruction because %RSP didn't change: no functions were called, and no registers were saved.

Disassembly of Optimized Executable

If we compile LocalVariables.cpp with the -O1 option, we see a very simple code that just returns zero:

```
(gdb) disass main
Dump of assembler code for function main:
=> 0x0000555555555125 <+0>:      mov     $0x0,%eax
   0x000055555555512a <+5>:      retq
End of assembler dump.
```

Where is all the code we have seen in the previous version? It was optimized away by the compiler because the results of our calculation are never used. Variables **a** and **b** are local to the *main* function, and their values are not accessible outside when we return from the function.

Summary

In this chapter, we looked into the stack layout of the more complex code: addressing arrays, local variables, and compiler-emitted code for the function prolog and epilog. Finally, we disassembled and analyzed code that used local variables and compared it to the optimized version.

The next chapter looks at function parameters and their stack layout. Finally, we disassemble and analyze another project with function parameters and local variables.

CHAPTER 11

Function Parameters

"FunctionParameters" Project

This chapter teaches how a caller function passes its parameters via registers and how a callee (the called function) accesses them. We use the following project that can be downloaded from this link:

github.com/apress/linux-debugging-disassembling-reversing/Chapter11/

Here is the project source code:

```
// FunctionParameters.cpp
int arithmetic (int a, int b);

int main(int argc, char* argv[])
{
    int result = arithmetic (1, 1);

return 0;
}

// Arithmetic.cpp
int arithmetic (int a, int b)
{
    b = b + a;
    ++a;
```

© Dmitry Vostokov 2023
D. Vostokov, *Foundations of Linux Debugging, Disassembling, and Reversing*,
https://doi.org/10.1007/978-1-4842-9153-5_11

```
    b = b * a;

    return b;
}
```

Stack Structure

Recall from the previous chapter that the %RBP register is used to address stack memory locations. It was illustrated in Figure 10-1. Here, we provide a typical example of the stack memory layout for the following function:

```
void func(int Param1, int Param2)
{
    int var1, var2;
    // stack memory layout at this point
// -0x18(%RBP) = Param2 (doubleword)
// -0x14(%RBP) = Param1 (doubleword)
// -0x8(%RBP) = var2 (doubleword)
// -0x4(%RBP) = var1 (doubleword)
// (%RBP)      = previous %RBP (quadword)
// 0x8(%RBP)   = return address (quadword)
// ...
}
```

The typical stack frame memory layout for the function with two arguments and two local variables is illustrated in Figure 11-1.

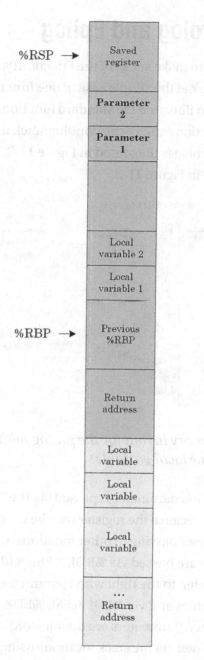

Figure 11-1. *Stack memory layout for the function with two arguments and two local variables*

Function Prolog and Epilog

Now, before we try to make sense of the FunctionParameters project disassembly, we look at the simple case of one function parameter and one local variable to illustrate the standard function prolog and epilog sequence of instructions and corresponding stack memory changes.

The function prolog is illustrated in Figure 11-2, and the function epilog is illustrated in Figure 11-3.

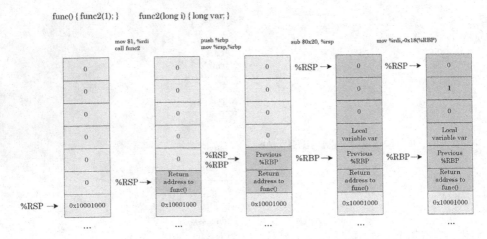

Figure 11-2. *Memory layout for the prolog with one function parameter and one local variable*

Here, the function parameter is passed via the %RDI register. It is saved on the stack because the register may be used later in calculations or function parameter passing to other functions. Generally, the function's first six parameters are passed via %RDI, %RSI, %RDX, %RCX, %R8, and %R9 registers from left to the right when parameters are quadwords like pointers or long values and via %EDI, %ESI, %EDX, %ECX, %R8D, and %R9D registers when parameters are doublewords like integers. Additional parameters are passed via the stack locations using the PUSH instruction.

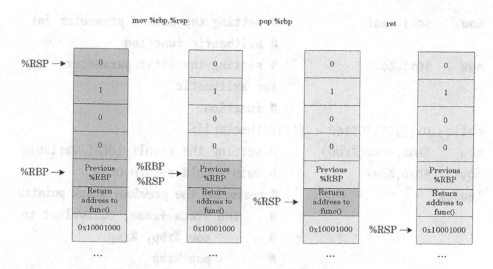

Figure 11-3. *Memory layout for the epilog with one function parameter and one local variable*

We also see that local variables are not initialized by default when their storage space is allocated via the SUB instruction and not cleared during the epilog. Whatever memory contents were there before allocation, it becomes the local variable values, the so-called garbage values.

Project Disassembled Code with Comments

Here is a commented code disassembly of *main* and *arithmetic* with memory addresses removed for visual clarity:

```
main:

push    %rbp                    # establishing stack frame
mov     %rsp,%rbp
sub     $0x20,%rsp              # creating stack frame for local
                                  variables and function parameters
mov     %edi,-0x14(%rbp)       # saving the first main parameter
mov     %rsi,-0x20(%rbp)       # saving the second main parameter
```

```
mov      $0x1,%esi              # setting the second parameter for
                                # arithmetic function
mov      $0x1,%edi              # setting the first parameter
                                for arithmetic
                                # function
callq    0x555555555514d <_Z10arithmeticii>
mov      %eax,-0x4(%rbp)        # setting the result local variable
mov      $0x0,%eax              # main should return 0
leaveq                          # restoring the previous stack pointer
                                #    and stack frame, equivalent to
                                #           mov %rbp, %rsp
                                #           pop %rbp

retq            # return from main

arithmetic:

push     %rbp                   # establishing stack frame
mov      %rsp,%rbp
mov      %edi,-0x4(%rbp)        # saving the first arithmetic
                                  parameter (a)
mov      %esi,-0x8(%rbp)        # saving the second arithmetic
                                  parameter (b)
mov      -0x4(%rbp),%eax        # (a) -> eax
add      %eax,-0x8(%rbp)        # eax + (b) -> (b)
addl     $0x1,-0x4(%rbp)        # 1 + (a) -> (a)
mov      -0x8(%rbp),%eax        # (b) -> eax
imul     -0x4(%rbp),%eax        # (a) * eax -> eax
mov      %eax,-0x8(%rbp)        # eax -> (b)
mov      -0x8(%rbp),%eax        # (b) -> eax
pop      %rbp                   # restoring the previous stack frame
                                #     no need to restore stack
                                      pointer as
```

```
                          #    it didn't change
retq                      # result value is in eax
```

We can put a breakpoint on the first arithmetic calculation address and examine raw stack data pointed to by the %RBP register:

```
coredump@DESKTOP-IS6V2LO:~/pflddr/x64/Chapter11$ gcc
FunctionParameters.cpp Arithmetic.cpp -o FunctionParameters
coredump@DESKTOP-IS6V2LO:~/pflddr/x64/Chapter11$ gdb
./FunctionParameters
GNU gdb (Debian 8.2.1-2+b3) 8.2.1
Copyright (C) 2018 Free Software Foundation, Inc.
License GPLv3+: GNU GPL version 3 or later <http://gnu.org/
licenses/gpl.html>
This is free software: you are free to change and
redistribute it.
There is NO WARRANTY, to the extent permitted by law.
Type "show copying" and "show warranty" for details.
This GDB was configured as "x86_64-linux-gnu".
Type "show configuration" for configuration details.
For bug reporting instructions, please see:
<http://www.gnu.org/software/gdb/bugs/>.
Find the GDB manual and other documentation resources
online at:
    <http://www.gnu.org/software/gdb/documentation/>.

For help, type "help".
Type "apropos word" to search for commands related to "word"...
Reading symbols from ./FunctionParameters...(no debugging
symbols found)...done.

(gdb) break main
Breakpoint 1 at 0x1129

(gdb) run
```

Starting program: /home/coredump/pflddr/x64/Chapter11/
FunctionParameters

Breakpoint 1, 0x0000555555555129 in main ()

(gdb) disass arithmetic
Dump of assembler code for function _Z10arithmeticii:
```
   0x000055555555514d <+0>:      push    %rbp
   0x000055555555514e <+1>:      mov     %rsp,%rbp
   0x0000555555555151 <+4>:      mov     %edi,-0x4(%rbp)
   0x0000555555555154 <+7>:      mov     %esi,-0x8(%rbp)
   0x0000555555555157 <+10>:     mov     -0x4(%rbp),%eax
   0x000055555555515a <+13>:     add     %eax,-0x8(%rbp)
   0x000055555555515d <+16>:     addl    $0x1,-0x4(%rbp)
   0x0000555555555161 <+20>:     mov     -0x8(%rbp),%eax
   0x0000555555555164 <+23>:     imul    -0x4(%rbp),%eax
   0x0000555555555168 <+27>:     mov     %eax,-0x8(%rbp)
   0x000055555555516b <+30>:     mov     -0x8(%rbp),%eax
   0x000055555555516e <+33>:     pop     %rbp
   0x000055555555516f <+34>:     retq
```
End of assembler dump.

(gdb) break *0x0000555555555157
Breakpoint 2 at 0x0000555555555157

(gdb) continue
Continuing.

Breakpoint 2, 0x0000555555555157 in arithmetic(int, int) ()

(gdb) info registers $rbp
rbp   0x7fffffffe500   0x7fffffffe500

(gdb) x/10a $rbp-0x20
0x7fffffffe4e0: 0x1   0x7ffff7eaaaf5 <handle_intel+197>

```
0x7ffffffffe4f0: 0x0          0x100000001                          ; (b, a)
0x7ffffffffe500: 0x7ffffffffe530    0x555555555143 <main+30> ;
saved $RBP, return address
0x7ffffffffe510: 0x7ffffffffe618    0x155555040
0x7ffffffffe520: 0x7ffffffffe610    0x0

(gdb) x/10w $rbp-0x20
0x7ffffffffe4e0: 0x1      0x0      0xffffffffff7eaaaf5    0x7fff
0x7ffffffffe4f0: 0x0      0x0      0x1       0x1       ; (b), (a)
0x7ffffffffe500: 0xffffffffffffffe530       0x7fff
```

Parameter Mismatch Problem

To illustrate the importance of understanding the stack memory layout,
consider this typical binary interface mismatch problem. The function
main calls *func* with two parameters:

```
// main.c
int main ()
{
    long locVar;
    func (1, 2);
    return 0;
}
```

The caller is expecting the callee function *func* to see this stack
memory layout and passes 1 in %RDI and 2 in %RSI:

```
        2
        1
        locVar
%RBP -> prev %RBP
        return address
```

However, the callee expects three parameters instead of two:

```c
// func.c
int func (int a, int b, int c)
{
    // code to use parameters
    return 0;
}
```

The *func* code sees this stack memory layout:

```
         (c)
         (b)
         (a)
         locVar
%RBP -> prev %RBP
         return address
```

We see that parameter **c** on the raw stack gets its value from some random value in %RDX that was never set by the caller. It is clearly a software defect (bug).

Summary

This chapter looked at function parameters and their stack layout. We disassembled and analyzed the stack structure of the project with function parameters and local variables. Finally, we looked at a parameter mismatch problem.

The next chapter is about CPU state flags, comparison instructions, conditional jumps, and function return values.

CHAPTER 12

More Instructions

CPU Flags Register

In addition to registers, the CPU also contains a 64-bit %RFLAGS register
where individual bits are set or cleared in response to arithmetic and
other operations. Separate machine instructions can manipulate some bit
values, and their values affect code execution.

For example, the DF bit (Direction Flag) determines the direction
of memory copy operations and can be set by STD and cleared by CLD
instructions. It has the default value of zero, and its location is shown in
Figure 12-1, where only the first 32 bits of 64-bit %RFLAGS are shown.

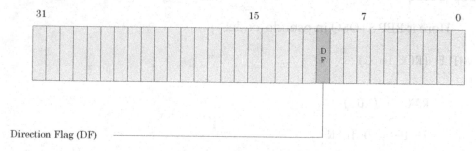

Figure 12-1. *%RFLAGS register flags*

© Dmitry Vostokov 2023
D. Vostokov, *Foundations of Linux Debugging, Disassembling, and Reversing,*
https://doi.org/10.1007/978-1-4842-9153-5_12

The Fast Way to Fill Memory

It can be done by the STOSQ instruction that stores a quadword value from %RAX into a memory location which address is in the %RDI register ("D" means destination). After the value from %RAX is transferred to memory, the instruction increments %RDI by eight, and if the DF flag is zero, %RDI now points to the next quadword in memory. If the DF flag is one, then the %RDI value is decremented by eight, and the %RDI now points to the previous quadword in memory. There is an equivalent STOSL instruction that stores doublewords and increments or decrements %RDI by four.

If we prefix any instruction with REP, it causes the instruction to be repeated until the %RCX register's value is decremented to zero. For example, we can write simple code that should theoretically zero "all memory" (practically, it traps because of access violation):

```
xor %rax, %rax              # fill with 0
mov $0, %rdi                # starting address or xor
                               %rdi, %rdi
mov $0xffffffff / 4, %rcx   # 0x1fffffff quad words
rep stosq
```

Here is REP STOSQ in pseudo-code:

```
WHILE (RCX != 0)
{
      RAX -> (RDI)

      IF DF = 0 THEN
            RDI + 8 -> RDI
      ELSE
            RDI - 8 -> RDI

      RCX - 1 -> RCX
}
```

A simple example of erasing 32 bytes (4x8) is shown in Figure 12-2.

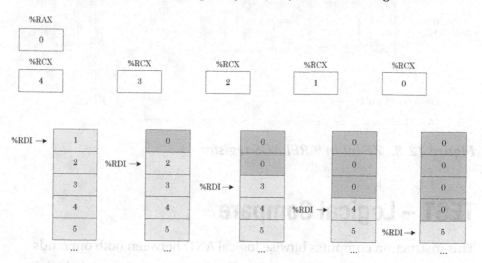

Figure 12-2. *A simple example of erasing 32 bytes*

Testing for 0

A ZF bit in the %RFLAGS register is set to one if the instruction result is zero and cleared otherwise. This bit is affected by

- Arithmetic instructions (e.g., ADD, SUB, MUL)

- Logical compare instruction (TEST)

- "Arithmetical" compare instruction (CMP)

The location of the ZF bit is shown in Figure 12-3.

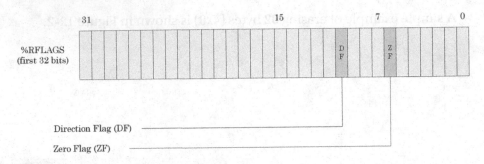

Figure 12-3. ZF bit in %RFLAGS register

TEST – Logical Compare

This instruction computes bitwise logical AND between both operands and sets flags (including ZF) according to the computed result (which is discarded):

TEST reg/imm, reg/mem

Examples:

TEST %EDX, %EDX

Suppose the %EDX register contains 4 (100_{bin}):

100_{bin} AND 100_{bin} = 100_{bin} != 0 (ZF is cleared)

TEST $1, $EDX

Suppose %EDX contains 0 (0_{bin}):

0_{bin} AND 1_{bin} = 0_{bin} == 0 (ZF is set)

Here is the TEST instruction in pseudo-code (details not relevant to the ZF bit are omitted):

TEMP := OPERAND1 AND OPERAND2

142

```
IF TEMP = 0 THEN
      1 -> ZF
ELSE
      0 -> ZF
```

CMP – Compare Two Operands

This instruction compares the first operand with the second and sets flags (including ZF) according to the computed result (which is discarded). The comparison is performed by subtracting the first operand from the second (like the SUB instruction: sub $4, %eax).

```
CMP reg/imm, reg/mem
CMP reg/mem/imm, reg
```

Examples:

```
CMP $0, %EDI
```

Suppose %EDI contains 0:

```
0 - 0   == 0 (ZF is set)
```

```
CMP $0x16, %EAX
```

Suppose %EAX contains 4_{hex}:

```
4hex - 16hex  = FFFFFFEEhex   != 0 (ZF is cleared)
4dec - 22dec  = -18dec
```

Here is the CMP instruction in pseudo-code (details not relevant to the ZF bit are omitted):

```
OPERAND2 - OPERAND1 -> TEMP
IF TEMP = 0 THEN
```

```
        1 -> ZF
ELSE
        0 -> ZF
```

The CMP instruction is equivalent to this pseudo-code sequence:

```
OPERAND2 -> TEMP
SUB OPERAND1, TEMP
```

TEST or CMP?

Both instructions are equivalent if we want to test for zero, but the CMP instruction affects more flags than TEST:

```
TEST %EAX, %EAX
CMP  $0, %EAX
```

The CMP instruction is used to compare for inequality (the TEST instruction cannot be used here):

```
CMP $0, %EAX    # > 0 or < 0 ?
```

The TEST instruction is used to see if individual bits are set:

```
TEST $2, %EAX   # 2 == 0010_{bin}  or in C language: if (var & 0x2)
```

Examples where %EAX has the value of 2:

```
TEST $4, %EAX   # 0010_{bin} AND 0100_{bin} = 0000_{bin} (ZF is set)
TEST $6, %EAX   # 0010_{bin} AND 0110_{bin} = 0010_{bin} (ZF is cleared)
```

Conditional Jumps

Consider these two C or C++ code fragments:

```
if (a == 0)                if (a != 0)
{                          {
    ++a;                       ++a;
}                          }
else                       else
{                          {
    --a;                       --a;
}                          }
```

The CPU fetches instructions sequentially, so we must tell the CPU that we want to skip some instructions if some condition is (not) met, for example, if a != 0.

JNZ (jump if not zero) and JZ (jump if zero) test the ZF flag and change %RIP if the ZF bit is cleared for JNZ or set for JZ. The following assembly language code is equivalent to the preceding C/C++ code:

```
        CMP    $0, A              MOV    A, %EAX
        JNZ    label1            TEST   %EAX, %EAX
        INC    A                  JZ     label1
        JMP    label2            INC    %EAX
label1: DEC    A                  JMP    label2
label2:                  label1: DEC    %EAX
                         label2:
```

The Structure of Registers

Some 64-bit registers have a legacy structure that allows us to address their lower 32-bit, 16-bit, and two 8-bit parts, as shown in Figure 12-4.

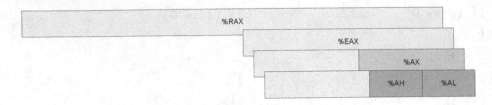

Figure 12-4. *A legacy structure of registers*

Function Return Value

Many functions return values via the %RAX register. For example:

long func();

The return value is in %RAX.

bool func();

The return value is in %EAX.

Although bool values occupy one byte in memory, the compiler may use %EAX instead of %AL.

Using Byte Registers

Suppose we have a byte value in the %AL register, and we want to add this value to the %ECX register. However, we do not know what values other parts of the full %EAX register contain. We cannot use this instruction, for example:

```
MOV   %AL, %EBX      # operand size conflict
```

The proposed solution in pseudo-code:

```
AL -> EBX           or    AL -> EAX
ECX + EBX -> ECX          ECX + EAX -> ECX
```

We can only use MOV instructions that have the same operand size for both source and destination, for example:

```
MOV    %AL, %BL
MOV    %AL, b        # in C: static bool b = func();
```

For this task, there is a special MOVZX (Move with Zero eXtend) instruction that replaces the contents of the second operand with the contents of the first operand while filling the rest of the bits with zeroes:

```
MOVZX reg/mem, reg
```

Therefore, our solution for the task becomes very simple:

```
MOVZX %AL, %EBX
ADD    %EBX, %ECX
```

We can also reuse the %EAX register:

```
MOVZX %AL, %EAX
ADD    %EAX, %ECX
```

Summary

In this chapter, we learned about CPU state flags, comparison instructions, conditional jumps, and function return values – usually present in real binary code that we may need to disassemble to understand program logic during debugging.

The next chapter is our "graduating" project – we disassemble and analyze a project that uses function parameters which are pointers.

CHAPTER 13

Function Pointer Parameters

"FunctionPointerParameters" Project

It is our final project, and it can be downloaded from

github.com/apress/linux-debugging-disassembling-reversing/
Chapter13/

A summary of the project source code:

```
// FunctionParameters.cpp
int main(int argc, char* argv[])
{
        int a, b;

        printf("Enter a and b: ");
        scanf("%d %d", &a, &b);

        if (arithmetic (a, &b))
        {
                printf("Result = %d", b);
        }

        return 0;
}
```

© Dmitry Vostokov 2023

D. Vostokov, *Foundations of Linux Debugging, Disassembling, and Reversing*,
https://doi.org/10.1007/978-1-4842-9153-5_13

```cpp
// Arithmetic.cpp
bool arithmetic (int a, int *b)
{
    if (!b)
    {
        return false;
    }

    *b = *b + a;
    ++a;
    *b = *b * a;

    return true;
}
```

Commented Disassembly

Here is the commented disassembly we get after compiling the project and loading into GDB:

coredump@DESKTOP-IS6V2LO:~/pflddr/x64/Chapter13$ gcc
FunctionParameters.cpp Arithmetic.cpp -o FunctionParameters

coredump@DESKTOP-IS6V2LO:~/pflddr/x64/Chapter13$ gdb
./FunctionParameters
GNU gdb (Debian 8.2.1-2+b3) 8.2.1
Copyright (C) 2018 Free Software Foundation, Inc.
License GPLv3+: GNU GPL version 3 or later <http://gnu.org/
licenses/gpl.html>
This is free software: you are free to change and
redistribute it.
There is NO WARRANTY, to the extent permitted by law.
Type "show copying" and "show warranty" for details.

This GDB was configured as "x86_64-linux-gnu".
Type "show configuration" for configuration details.
For bug reporting instructions, please see:
<http://www.gnu.org/software/gdb/bugs/>.
Find the GDB manual and other documentation resources
online at:
    <http://www.gnu.org/software/gdb/documentation/>.

For help, type "help".
Type "apropos word" to search for commands related to "word"...
Reading symbols from ./FunctionParameters...(no debugging
symbols found)...done.

(gdb) break main
Breakpoint 1 at 0x1149

(gdb) run
Starting program: /home/coredump/pflddr/x64/Chapter13/
FunctionParameters

Breakpoint 1, 0x0000555555555149 in main ()

(gdb) disass main
Dump of assembler code for function main:
   0x0000555555555145 <+0>:   push   %rbp
   0x0000555555555146 <+1>:   mov   %rsp,%rbp
=> 0x0000555555555149 <+4>:   sub $0x20,%rsp
   0x000055555555514d <+8>:   mov   %edi,-0x14(%rbp)
   0x0000555555555150 <+11>:   mov   %rsi,-0x20(%rbp)
   0x0000555555555154 <+15>:   lea   0xea9(%rip),%rdi
   # 0x555555556004
   0x000055555555515b <+22>:   mov $0x0,%eax
   0x0000555555555160 <+27>:   callq 0x555555555030
                                <printf@plt>

```
0x0000555555555165 <+32>:    lea    -0x8(%rbp),%rdx
0x0000555555555169 <+36>:    lea    -0x4(%rbp),%rax
0x000055555555516d <+40>:    mov    %rax,%rsi
0x0000555555555170 <+43>:    lea    0xe9d(%rip),%rdi
# 0x555555556014
0x0000555555555177 <+50>:    mov    $0x0,%eax
0x000055555555517c <+55>:    callq  0x555555555040
                                    <scanf@plt>
0x0000555555555181 <+60>:    mov    -0x4(%rbp),%eax
0x0000555555555184 <+63>:    lea    -0x8(%rbp),%rdx
0x0000555555555188 <+67>:    mov    %rdx,%rsi
0x000055555555518b <+70>:    mov    %eax,%edi
0x000055555555518d <+72>:    callq  0x5555555551b3
                                    <_Z10arithmeticiPi>
0x0000555555555192 <+77>:    test   %al,%al
0x0000555555555194 <+79>:    je     0x5555555551ac
                                    <main+103>
0x0000555555555196 <+81>:    mov    -0x8(%rbp),%eax
0x0000555555555199 <+84>:    mov    %eax,%esi
0x000055555555519b <+86>:    lea    0xe78(%rip),%rdi
# 0x55555555601a
0x00005555555551a2 <+93>:    mov    $0x0,%eax
0x00005555555551a7 <+98>:    callq  0x555555555030
                                    <printf@plt>
0x00005555555551ac <+103>:   mov    $0x0,%eax
0x00005555555551b1 <+108>:   leaveq
0x00005555555551b2 <+109>:   retq
End of assembler dump.

(gdb) x/s 0x555555556004
0x555555556004: "Enter a and b: "
```

```
(gdb) x/s 0x555555556014
0x555555556014: "%d %d"

(gdb) x/s 0x55555555601a
0x55555555601a: "Result = %d"

(gdb) disass arithmetic
Dump of assembler code for function _Z10arithmeticiPi:
   0x00005555555551b3 <+0>:    push   %rbp
   0x00005555555551b4 <+1>:    mov    %rsp,%rbp
   0x00005555555551b7 <+4>:    mov    %edi,-0x4(%rbp)
   0x00005555555551ba <+7>:    mov    %rsi,-0x10(%rbp)
   0x00005555555551be <+11>:   cmpq   $0x0,-0x10(%rbp)
   0x00005555555551c3 <+16>:   jne    0x5555555551cc
                                      <_Z10arithmeticiPi+25>
   0x00005555555551c5 <+18>:   mov    $0x0,%eax
   0x00005555555551ca <+23>:   jmp    0x5555555551f8
                                      <_Z10arithmeticiPi+69>
   0x00005555555551cc <+25>:   mov    -0x10(%rbp),%rax
   0x00005555555551d0 <+29>:   mov    (%rax),%edx
   0x00005555555551d2 <+31>:   mov    -0x4(%rbp),%eax
   0x00005555555551d5 <+34>:   add    %eax,%edx
   0x00005555555551d7 <+36>:   mov    -0x10(%rbp),%rax
   0x00005555555551db <+40>:   mov    %edx,(%rax)
   0x00005555555551dd <+42>:   addl   $0x1,-0x4(%rbp)
   0x00005555555551e1 <+46>:   mov    -0x10(%rbp),%rax
   0x00005555555551e5 <+50>:   mov    (%rax),%eax
   0x00005555555551e7 <+52>:   imul   -0x4(%rbp),%eax
   0x00005555555551eb <+56>:   mov    %eax,%edx
   0x00005555555551ed <+58>:   mov    -0x10(%rbp),%rax
   0x00005555555551f1 <+62>:   mov    %edx,(%rax)
   0x00005555555551f3 <+64>:   mov    $0x1,%eax
```

```
    0x00005555555551f8 <+69>:    pop     %rbp
    0x00005555555551f9 <+70>:    retq
End of assembler dump.
```

main:

push   %rbp   # establishing
                                                         stack frame

mov   %rsp,%rbp
sub $0x20,%rsp   # creating
                                                         stack frame
                                                         for locals
                                                         #   and main
                                                         function
                                                         parameters

mov   %edi,-0x14(%rbp)   # saving the
                                                         first main
                                                         parameter

mov   %rsi,-0x20(%rbp)   # saving the
                                                         second main
                                                         parameter

lea   0xea9(%rip),%rdi   # 0x555555556004   # the address
                                                         of printf
                                                         #   string
                                                         parameter

mov $0x0,%eax
callq   0x555555555030 <printf@plt>   # printf
                                                         ("Enter a
                                                         and b: ")

lea   -0x8(%rbp),%rdx   # address b
                                                         -> rdx (3rd
                                                         parameter)

154

```
lea     -0x4(%rbp),%rax                                      # address
                                                             a -> rax
mov     %rax,%rsi                                            #       rax
                                                             -> rsi (2nd
                                                             parameter)
lea     0xe9d(%rip),%rdi        # 0x555555556014            # the
                                                             address of
                                                             scanf string
                                                             #   parameter
                                                             (1st parameter)
mov     $0x0,%eax
callq   0x555555555040 <scanf@plt>                          # scanf("%d
                                                             %d", &a, &b)
                                                             #   parameters
                                                             are passed via
                                                             %rdi,
                                                             %rsi, %rdx
mov     -0x4(%rbp),%eax                                      # (a) -> eax
                                                             (value of a)
lea     -0x8(%rbp),%rdx                                      # address
                                                             b -> rdx
mov     %rdx,%rsi                                            #       rdx
                                                             -> rsi (2nd
                                                             parameter)
mov     %eax,%edi                                            # eax ->
                                                             edi ((a), 1st
                                                             parameter)

callq   0x5555555551b3 <_Z10arithmeticiPi>                  # arithmetic
                                                             (a, &b)
test    %al,%al                                              # tesing
                                                             for zero
```

```
                                              #     bool
                                              result from
                                              arithmetic
je      0x5555555551ac <main+103>             # if = 0
                                              #   0x000055555
                                              55551ac -> rip
mov     -0x8(%rbp),%eax                       # (b) -> eax
                                              (value of b)
mov     %eax,%esi                             #      eax ->
                                              esi  (2nd
                                              parameter)
lea     0xe78(%rip),%rdi    # 0x55555555601a  # the address
                                              of printf
                                              #     string
                                              parameter
mov     $0x0,%eax
callq   0x555555555030 <printf@plt>           # printf
                                              ("Result
                                              = %d", b)

0x00005555555551ac <+103>:
mov     $0x0,%eax                             # main should
                                              return 0
leaveq                                        # restoring
                                              the previous
                                              #     stack
                                              pointer and
                                              #     stack
                                              frame,
                                              equivalent to
                                              #      mov
                                              %rbp, %rsp
                                              #     pop %rbp
```

```
retq                                                # return
                                                    from main

arithmetic:

push   %rbp                                         # establishing
                                                    stack frame

mov    %rsp,%rbp
mov    %edi,-0x4(%rbp)                              # saving the
                                                    first
                                                    parameter (p1)
mov    %rsi,-0x10(%rbp)                             # saving
                                                    the second
                                                    parameter (p2)

cmpq   $0x0,-0x10(%rbp)                             # if p2 != 0
jne    0x5555555551cc <_Z10arithmeticiPi+25>        #   goto
                                                    0x555555
                                                    5551cc

mov    $0x0,%eax                                    # return
                                                    value 0

jmp    0x5555555551f8 <_Z10arithmeticiPi+69>        # goto epilog
0x00005555555551cc <+25>:
mov    -0x10(%rbp),%rax                             # (p2) -> rax
mov    (%rax),%edx                                  # (rax) ->
                                                    edx (*p2)
                                                    #   p2 is
                                                    a pointer
                                                    since it
                                                    #   contains
                                                    the address of
                                                    #   variable
                                                    that we name b
```

```
mov     -0x4(%rbp),%eax
add     %eax,%edx


mov     -0x10(%rbp),%rax

mov     %edx,(%rax)


addl    $0x1,-0x4(%rbp)

mov     -0x10(%rbp),%rax

mov     (%rax),%eax
imul    -0x4(%rbp),%eax

mov     %eax,%edx
mov     -0x10(%rbp),%rax

mov     %edx,(%rax)


mov     $0x1,%eax

0x00005555555551f8 <+69>:
pop     %rbp
```

```
# we also
name p1 as a
# (a) -> eax
# eax +
edx -> edx
#   (a) +
(b) -> edx
# address
b -> rax
# edx -> (b)
#   (a) +
(b) -> (b)
# 1 +
(a) -> (a)
# address
b -> rax
# (b) -> eax
# (a) * (b)
-> eax
# eax -> edx
# address
b -> rax
# edx -> (b)
#   (a) *
(b) -> (b)
# 1 -> eax
(return value)

# restoring
the previous
stack frame
```

```
                                        #      no need
                                        to restore
                                        #      stack
                                        pointer as
                                        #      it
                                        didn't change
retq                                    # result value
                                        is in eax
```

Summary

In this chapter, we disassembled and analyzed a project that used function parameters which are pointers.

The next, final chapter of the book summarizes various basic disassembly patterns.

CHAPTER 14

Summary of Code Disassembly Patterns

This final chapter summarizes the various patterns we have encountered during the reading of this book.

Function Prolog/Epilog

Function prolog

```
push    %rbp
mov     %rsp,%rbp
```

Function epilog

```
mov     %rbp,%rsp
pop     %rbp
ret
```

It is equivalent to

```
leave
ret
```

Some code may omit to restore %RSP if it does not change:

```
pop     %rbp
ret
```

© Dmitry Vostokov 2023
D. Vostokov, *Foundations of Linux Debugging, Disassembling, and Reversing*,
https://doi.org/10.1007/978-1-4842-9153-5_14

Knowing prolog can help identify situations when symbol files or function start addresses are not correct. For example, suppose we have the following backtrace:

```
func3+0x5F
func2+0x8F
func+0x20
```

If we disassemble the *func2* function and see that it does not start with prolog, we may assume that backtrace needs more attention:

```
(gdb) x/2i func2
0x555555555165 <main+32>:    lea    -0x8(%rbp),%rdx
0x555555555169 <main+36>:    lea    -0x4(%rbp),%rax
```

In optimized code, the %RSP register may be used to address local variables and parameters instead of %RBP. In such a case, prolog and epilog may be partially missing. Here is an example from the *printf* function:

```
(gdb) disass printf
Dump of assembler code for function __printf:
   0x00007ffff7e60560 <+0>:     sub    $0xd8,%rsp
   0x00007ffff7e60567 <+7>:     mov    %rsi,0x28(%rsp)
   0x00007ffff7e6056c <+12>:    mov    %rdx,0x30(%rsp)
   0x00007ffff7e60571 <+17>:    mov    %rcx,0x38(%rsp)
   0x00007ffff7e60576 <+22>:    mov    %r8,0x40(%rsp)
   0x00007ffff7e6057b <+27>:    mov    %r9,0x48(%rsp)
   0x00007ffff7e60580 <+32>:    test   %al,%al
   0x00007ffff7e60582 <+34>:    je     0x7ffff7e605bb <__
                                       printf+91>
   0x00007ffff7e60584 <+36>:    movaps %xmm0,0x50(%rsp)
   0x00007ffff7e60589 <+41>:    movaps %xmm1,0x60(%rsp)
   0x00007ffff7e6058e <+46>:    movaps %xmm2,0x70(%rsp)
```

```
0x00007ffff7e60593 <+51>:     movaps  %xmm3,0x80(%rsp)
0x00007ffff7e6059b <+59>:     movaps  %xmm4,0x90(%rsp)
0x00007ffff7e605a3 <+67>:     movaps  %xmm5,0xa0(%rsp)
0x00007ffff7e605ab <+75>:     movaps  %xmm6,0xb0(%rsp)
0x00007ffff7e605b3 <+83>:     movaps  %xmm7,0xc0(%rsp)
0x00007ffff7e605bb <+91>:     mov     %fs:0x28,%rax
0x00007ffff7e605c4 <+100>:    mov     %rax,0x18(%rsp)
0x00007ffff7e605c9 <+105>:    xor     %eax,%eax
0x00007ffff7e605cb <+107>:    lea     0xe0(%rsp),%rax
0x00007ffff7e605d3 <+115>:    mov     %rdi,%rsi
0x00007ffff7e605d6 <+118>:    mov     %rsp,%rdx
0x00007ffff7e605d9 <+121>:    mov     %rax,0x8(%rsp)
0x00007ffff7e605de <+126>:    lea     0x20(%rsp),%rax
0x00007ffff7e605e3 <+131>:    mov     %rax,0x10(%rsp)
0x00007ffff7e605e8 <+136>:    mov     0x162959(%rip),%rax
           # 0x7ffff7fc2f48
0x00007ffff7e605ef <+143>:    movl    $0x8,(%rsp)
0x00007ffff7e605f6 <+150>:    mov     (%rax),%rdi
0x00007ffff7e605f9 <+153>:    movl    $0x30,0x4(%rsp)
0x00007ffff7e60601 <+161>:    callq   0x7ffff7e579f0 <_IO_
                                       vfprintf_internal>
0x00007ffff7e60606 <+166>:    mov     0x18(%rsp),%rcx
0x00007ffff7e6060b <+171>:    xor     %fs:0x28,%rcx
0x00007ffff7e60614 <+180>:    jne     0x7ffff7e6061e <__
                                       printf+190>
0x00007ffff7e60616 <+182>:    add     $0xd8,%rsp
0x00007ffff7e6061d <+189>:    retq
0x00007ffff7e6061e <+190>:    callq   0x7ffff7f127b0 <__stack_
                                       chk_fail>
```

End of assembler dump.

LEA (Load Effective Address)

The following instruction

```
lea     -0x8(%rbp),%rdx
```

is equivalent to the following arithmetic sequence:

```
mov     %rbp, %rdx
add     -0x8, %rdx
```

The following instruction

```
lea     0xea9(%rip),%rdi
```

is equivalent to the following arithmetic sequence:

```
mov     %rip, %rdi
add     0xea9, %rdi
```

Passing Parameters

The first six function parameters from left to right

%RDI, %RSI, %RDX, %RCX, %R8, and %R9

Note   Although we haven't seen examples for more than six function parameters, they are passed via the stack, for example, via the PUSH instruction.

Static/global variable address (or string constant)

```
mov     $0x555555556004, reg
lea     0xe9d(%rip), reg
```

Local variable value vs. local variable address

```
mov    -XXX(%rbp), reg        ; local variable value
call   func

lea    -XXX(%rbp), reg        ; local variable address
call   func
```

Accessing Parameters and Local Variables

Local variable value

```
mov -XXX(%rbp), reg
mov XXX(%rsp), reg            # optimized code
```

Local variable address

```
lea -XXX(%rbp), reg
lea XXX(%rsp), reg            # optimized code
```

Accessing a doubleword value

```
mov    -0x8(%rbp), %eax
add    $1, %eax
addl   $1, %rax
```

Accessing a quadword value

```
mov    -0x8(%rbp), %rax
add    $1, %rax
```

Accessing and dereferencing a pointer to a doubleword value

```
mov    -0x10(%rbp), %rax
mov    (%rax), %eax
add    $1, %eax
```

Accessing and dereferencing a pointer to a quadword value

```
mov     -0x10(%rbp), %rax
mov     (%rax), %rax
add     $1, %rax
```

Optimized code may not use stack locations to address function parameters (use only registers through which the parameters were passed) as can be seen in the previous chapter's example compiled with the -O1 switch:

```
(gdb) disass arithmetic
Dump of assembler code for function _Z10arithmeticiPi:
   0x00005555555551ab <+0>:     test   %rsi,%rsi
   0x00005555555551ae <+3>:     je     0x5555555551c2
                                       <_Z10arithmeticiPi+23>
   0x00005555555551b0 <+5>:     mov    %edi,%eax
   0x00005555555551b2 <+7>:     add    (%rsi),%eax
   0x00005555555551b4 <+9>:     add    $0x1,%edi
   0x00005555555551b7 <+12>:    imul   %eax,%edi
   0x00005555555551ba <+15>:    mov    %edi,(%rsi)
   0x00005555555551bc <+17>:    mov    $0x1,%eax
   0x00005555555551c1 <+22>:    retq
   0x00005555555551c2 <+23>:    mov    $0x0,%eax
   0x00005555555551c7 <+28>:    retq
End of assembler dump.
```

Summary

This chapter can be used as a reference to basic disassembly patterns.

Index

A

Access violation, 65, 66, 140
ADD, 5, 9–11, 13, 16, 43, 46, 49, 81,
        141, 146, 147, 165, 166
ADDL, 43, 81
ADDQ, 81
AL, 146, 147
AND, 82, 142, 144
Application crash, 65
Application memory, 105
Arithmetic project
    adding numbers to memory
        cells, 8, 10, 11
    assigning numbers to memory
        locations, 5–7
    C/C++ program, 19, 20
    computer program, 5
    contents at memory address, 4
    increment by one, 5
    memory layout and
        registers, 3, 4
Assembly language
        instructions, 81
Assignment, 6

B

Backtrace, 114, 162
Base pointer, 118
Binary notation, 30
Binary representation, 29
Bit granularity
    unsigned char, 54
    unsigned int, 55
    unsigned long, 55
    unsigned long long, 55
    unsigned short, 54
Breakpoint, 22, 38, 113, 125, 135
break command, 22, 38, 70, 88, 125,
        135, 136, 151
bt command, 114
Byte granularity, 53, 54

C

CALL, 100, 108–110, 117
Callee, 110, 129, 137
Caller, 110, 111, 123, 137, 138
Call stack, 110, 111
C and C++ compilers, 65

Printed in the United States
by Baker & Taylor Publisher Services